Butterflies
of the Midwest
Field Guide

Jaret C. Daniels

PUBLICATIONS
adventure
an imprint of Adventure**KEEN**

ACKNOWLEDGMENTS

I would like to thank my wife Stephanie, for her unconditional love and support. Thanks also to my parents for their enduring encouragement of my interest in natural history and all things wild.

Edited by Jenna Barron and Brett Ortler

Proofread by Ritchey Halphen

Cover and book design by Jonathan Norberg

Illustrations by Julie Martinez

Cover photo: Viceroy by Kevin Collison/shutterstock
Back cover and pg. 396 author photo: University of Florida/Brianne Lehan
Some images identified left to right in descending positions a, b, c, d, e, f, g, h; i=inset
All photos by Jaret C. Daniels except when noted.

All photos copyright of their prospective photographers:
Annette Allor: 56; **Matthew Brust:** 254; **Cory Gregory:** 205; **Frode Jacobsen:** 108; **Norbert Kondla:** 160; **Kathy Malone:** 155

Images used under license from Shutterstock.com.
aabeele: 36i; **Erik Agar:** 104; **alpi25:** 276i; **John A. Anderson:** 14c; **LABETAA Andre:** 312i; **Agnieszka Bacal:** 388b; **Gualberto Becerra:** 15c; **Randy Bjorklund:** 230i; **South O Boy:** 284; **chiltern-green.de:** 312; **Kevin Collison:** 336i-2; 338; **Mircea Costina:** 18b, 19b, 44; **Adventuring Dave:** 389h; **Gerald A. DeBoer:** 68i, 106, 136, 248; **Danita Delimont:** 356, 38i-2, 290, 296i; **Lee Ellsworth:** 118; **Isabel Eve:** 389b; **Melinda Fawver:** 252, 360; **Tyler Fox:** 50i, 388c; **Cameala Freed:** 18a; **Hanley CHDPhoto:** 374; **Tyler Hartl:** 334; **David Havel:** 348; **Maria T Hoffman:** 274; **Brett Hondow:** 232i, 246i, 284i; **Kim Howell:** 12; **IN Dancing Light:** 42i; **Jukka Jantunen:** 250; **Andy Jenner:** 20b; **Matt Jeppson:** 388d; **JMCA.photo:** 208i; **Steve Jordan:** 17a; **Rosemarie Kappler:** 14a; **Breck P. Kent:** 348i, 386; **Tomasz Klejdysz:** 389f; **Brian Lasenby:** 1/c, 196i, 332, 382; **laura.h:** 16c, 200i; **Doug Lemke:** 202i, 272i; **LorraineHudgins:** 177, 218; **Rose Ludwig:** 389d; **Mabeline72:** 19c; **Russell Marshall:** 289; **Kyle R. Mayfield:** 336i-1; **T. M. McCarthy:** 48i; **Michael G McKinne:** 13, 272; **Roger Meerts:** 268i; **Petr Muckstein:** 228i; **Matthew L Niemiller:** 320; **Sari ONeal:** 94, 132i, 240, 297i, 389a; **Jay Ondreicka:** 20d, 350, 370, 389g; **Massimiliano Paolino:** 389e;

photo credits continued on page 394

10 9 8 7 6 5 4 3 2

Butterflies of the Midwest Field Guide
Copyright © 2023 by Jaret C. Daniels
Published by Adventure Publications
An imprint of AdventureKEEN
310 Garfield Street South
Cambridge, Minnesota 55008
(800) 678-7006
www.adventurepublications.net
All rights reserved
Printed in China
LCCN 2022059610 (print); 2022059611 (ebook)
ISBN 978-1-64755-285-5 (pbk.); ISBN 978-1-64755-286-2 (ebook)

TABLE OF CONTENTS

WATCHING BUTTERFLIES AND MOTHS IN THE MIDWEST

People are rapidly discovering the joy of butterfly gardening and watching. Both are simple, fun, and rewarding ways to explore the natural world and bring the beauty of nature closer. Few other forms of wildlife are more attractive or as easily observed as butterflies and moths. They occur just about everywhere, from suburban gardens and urban parks to rural meadows and remote natural areas. Regardless of where you may live, there are a variety of butterflies and moths to be seen.

Butterflies of the Midwest is for anyone who wishes to identify and learn more about the butterflies found in our region, which covers Illinois, Indiana, Iowa, Kansas, Michigan, Minnesota, Missouri, Nebraska, North Dakota, Ohio, South Dakota, and Wisconsin.

There are more than 800 species of butterflies in North America north of Mexico, and around 11,000 moth species. While the majority of these are regular breeding residents, others show up from time to time as rare tropical strays. In the Midwest, around 200 different butterflies have been recorded. Within this mix, there are some that occur commonly over a large portion of the continent and others that are rare or limited to only a few areas, including four species federally listed as threatened or endangered.

Although such numbers pale in comparison to many tropical countries, the region boasts a rich and diverse butterfly and moth fauna—a unique bounty that is just waiting to be enjoyed! This book contains more than 170 species of butterflies, as well as more than two dozen moth species.

In total area (land and water), the Midwest covers some 750,000 square miles, a huge amount of space that includes tens of thousands of miles of shoreline, thousands of miles of Great

Lakes coastline, and tens of thousands of lakes, ponds, streams, and rivers. (Minnesota alone has more than 11,000 lakes.)

The region extends over 1,300 miles from the rolling hills of the Appalachian Plateau in southeast Ohio to the mixed-grass prairie of western Nebraska. Similarly, one could travel some 1,155 miles from the wetlands of the Mississippi Alluvial Plain in southern Missouri to the peatlands of northern Minnesota and the Northwest Angle, otherwise known as the northernmost point in the Lower 48 States. As a result, the Midwest's climate varies considerably, with the mean minimum annual winter temperatures of the northern and southern counties differing by more than 40 degrees Fahrenheit and encompassing a huge climactic range. (The USDA Plant Hardiness Zones in the Midwest range from 7b to 3a.)

Collectively, the region comprises more than seven physiographic provinces and an amazing diversity of different natural communities that are too numerous to fully list. These include open systems dominated by herbaceous plants such as tallgrass prairie, marsh, fen, bog, and dune; heavily wooded systems, including floodplain forest, upland deciduous forest, wooded swamp, and coniferous forest; and semiopen systems such as rocky outcrops, cliffs, and savannas that may contain a partial tree canopy or scattered shrubs along with open areas dominated by herbaceous vegetation. This diversity is driven by climate, location, topography, soil, and past geological activity. The end result is that this rich array of systems supports an equally rich butterfly fauna, including some that are extremely localized and habitat restricted.

The Midwest is at the crossroads of a wonderful mix of butterfly ranges, hosting those with true northern affinities, including some mostly found in Canada and its boreal forests, and welcoming others with more-southern tastes. The region also hosts a number of predominantly western species that just cross into our borders. For butterfly enthusiasts, it's hard to ask for much more. Get outside and enjoy the Midwest's natural riches!

WHAT ARE BUTTERFLIES?

Butterflies and moths are insects. Together, they compose the order Lepidoptera, a combination of Greek words meaning "scale-winged," and they can be differentiated from all other insects on that basis. Their four wings, as well as their body, are typically almost entirely covered with numerous tiny scales. Overlapping like shingles on a roof, they make up the color and pattern of a butterfly's wings. Although generally wide and flat, some scales may be modified in shape, depending on the species and body location.

Butterflies and moths are closely related and often difficult to quickly tell apart. Nonetheless, there are some basic differences that are easy to identify even in the field.

Generally, butterflies fly during the day, have large colorful wings that are held vertically together over the back when at rest, and bear distinctly clubbed antennae. In contrast, most moths are nocturnal. They are usually drabber in color overall and may often resemble dirty, hairy butterflies. At rest, they tend to hold their wings to the sides, and they have feathery or threadlike antennae.

The following illustration points out the basic parts of a butterfly or a moth.

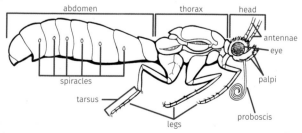

BUTTERFLY AND MOTH BASICS

Adult butterflies and moths share several common characteristics, including six jointed legs, two compound eyes, two antennae, a hard exoskeleton, and three main body segments: the head, thorax, and abdomen.

Head

The head has two large compound eyes, two long antennae, a proboscis, and two labial palpi. The rounded compound eyes are composed of hundreds of tiny, individually lensed eyes. Together, they render a single, somewhat pixelated color image. Adult butterflies have good vision and are able to distinguish light in both the visible and ultraviolet range. Unlike butterflies, most moths are primarily nocturnal. As a result of living in this low-light world, they've adapted to have eyes that favor contrast sensitivity at the expense of resolution.

Above the eyes are two, generally long antennae. In butterflies, these are clubbed at the tip. By contrast, moths may have several different antennal types ranging from thread-like to feathery. They bear various sensory structures that help with orientation and smell. At the front of the head, below the eyes, are two protruding, hairy, brush-like structures called labial palpi. They serve to house and protect the proboscis, or tongue. The proboscis is a long, flexible, straw-like structure used for drinking fluids. It can be tightly coiled below the head or extended when feeding.

The length and structure of proboscis determines the types of flowers and other foods from which it may feed. Some moths lack functional mouthparts and do not feed as adults.

Thorax

Directly behind the head is the thorax. It is a large, muscular portion divided into three segments that bear six legs and four wings. Each leg is jointed and contains five separate sections, the last of which is the tarsus (plural tarsi) or foot, which bears a tiny, hooked claw at the end. In addition to enabling the insect to securely grasp leaves, branches, or other objects, the tarsi have sensory structures that are used to taste. Adult females scratch a leaf surface with their front tarsi to release the leaf's chemicals and taste whether they have found the correct host plant. Above the legs are two pairs of wings. Made up of two thin membranes supported by rigid veins, the generally large, colorful wings are covered with millions of tiny scales that overlap like shingles on a roof. The wings serve a variety of critical functions, including flight, thermoregulation, sex recognition, camouflage, mimicry, and predator deflection.

Abdomen

The last section of a butterfly or moth's body is the elongated abdomen. In butterflies, the abdomen is typically slender, while it may be more robust in some moths. It is composed of 10 segments and contains the reproductive, digestive, and excretory systems along with a series of small lateral holes, called spiracles, for air exchange. The reproductive organs or genitalia are located at the end of the abdomen. Male butterflies and moths have two modified structures called claspers that are used to grasp the female during copulation. Females possess a genital opening for mating and a second opening for egg laying. While these structures are often difficult to see in certain species, females generally have a much larger, fatter-looking abdomen because they carry a large complement of eggs.

Wing Features

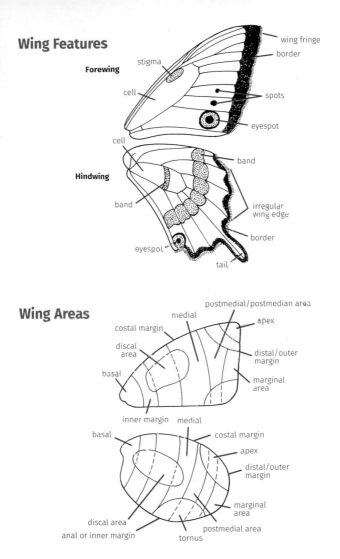

Forewing

stigma

wing fringe

border

cell

spots

eyespot

Hindwing

cell

band

band

irregular wing edge

border

eyespot

tail

Wing Areas

postmedial/postmedian area

medial

apex

costal margin

discal area

distal/outer margin

basal

marginal area

inner margin   medial

basal

costal margin

apex

distal/outer margin

marginal area

discal area

postmedial area

anal or inner margin

tornus

THE BUTTERFLY AND MOTH LIFE CYCLE

All butterflies and moths pass through a life cycle consisting of four developmental stages: egg, larva, pupa, and adult.

Regardless of size, adults begin life as a small egg. A female may lay her eggs singly, in small clusters, or in large groupings on or near the appropriate host plant. Once an egg hatches, the tiny larva begins feeding almost immediately. Butterfly and moth larvae are herbivores—with the exception of Harvester Butterfly larvae, which eat aphids—and they essentially live to eat. As a result, they can grow at an astonishing rate. All insects, including butterflies and moths, have an external skeleton. In order to grow, a developing caterpillar (or larva) must shed its skin, or molt, several times during its life. Each time the larva does, it discards its old, tight skin to make room for the new, roomier, and often different looking skin underneath. These different stages in a caterpillar's growth are called instars. Once fully grown, the larva stops eating and seeks a safe place

Monarch Butterfly Life Cycle

1. egg
2. caterpillar
3–4. creating the chrysalis
5–6. metamorphosis occurring within the chrysalis
7. adult emerges
8. adult butterfly

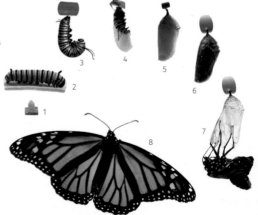

to pupate. It usually attaches itself to a branch, twig, or other surface with silk and molts for the last time to reveal the pupa (or chrysalis). Many moths spin silken cocoons to enclose their pupae. Inside, the larval structures are broken down and reorganized into the form of an adult insect. At the appropriate time, the pupa splits open and a beautiful new butterfly or moth emerges. The adult hangs quietly and begins to expand its crumpled wings by slowly forcing blood through the veins. After a few hours, its wings are fully hardened and the butterfly or moth is ready to fly.

BUTTERFLY FAMILIES

Butterflies can be divided into five major families: Hesperiidae, Lycaenidae, Nymphalidae, Papilionidae, and Pieridae. The members of each family have certain basic characteristics and behaviors that can be useful for identification. Keep in mind that the features listed are only generalities, and that there may be individual exceptions.

Hesperiidae: Skippers

Skippers are small- to medium-sized butterflies with robust, hairy bodies and relatively compact wings. They are generally brown, orange, or white, and their antennae bear short, distinct hooks at the tip. Adults have a quick and erratic flight, usually low to the ground. There are four main subfamilies: banded skippers, intermediate skipper, giant-skippers, and spread-wing skippers.

Banded skippers (Subfamily Hesperiinae) are small, brown or orange butterflies with somewhat pointed forewings. Many have dark markings or distinct black forewing stigmas. They readily visit flowers and hold their wings together over the back while feeding. Adults often perch or rest in a characteristic posture

with forewings held partially open and hindwings separated and lowered further.

Intermediate skippers (Subfamily Heteropterinae) are a rather small, brown or orange butterflies. Many have distinctive spot patterns and lack the short extension at the tip of the antennae (called the apiculus) that characterize other skippers. The adults have a relatively low, weak flight and bask with wings partially open.

As their name suggests, ***giant-skippers*** (Subfamily Megathyminae) dwarf most other members of the family. They are medium-sized brown butterflies with yellow markings and thick, robust bodies. The adults have a fast and rapid flight. Males establish territories and generally perch on low vegetation. Adults do not visit flowers.

Spread-wing skippers (Subfamily Pyrginae) are generally dark, dull-colored butterflies with wide wings. Most have small, light spots on the forewings. Some species have hindwing tails. The adults often feed, rest, and perch with their wings outstretched. They readily visit flowers.

Lycaenidae: Gossamer Wings

This diverse family includes coppers, harvesters, blues, hairstreaks, and metalmarks. The adults are small and often brilliantly colored but easily overlooked. Throughout the region, blues and hairstreaks predominate, with only one harvester, two metalmarks, and six coppers.

Coppers (Subfamily Lycaeninae) are small, sexually dimorphic butterflies (males and females look different). The upper

wing surfaces of most species are ornately colored with metallic reddish orange or purple. Many eastern species are associated with bogs, wet meadows and marshes. Populations are often quite localized but may be numerous when encountered. Adults typically scurry close to the ground with a quick flight, and they frequently visit available flowers or perch on low-growing vegetation with their wings held partially open.

The **harvester** (Subfamily Miletinae) is the only North American member of this unique, primarily European subfamily. It is our only butterfly with carnivorous larvae. Instead of feeding on plants, the larvae devour woolly aphids. The adults do not visit flowers but sip honeydew, a sugary secretion produced by their host aphids.

Aptly named, **blues** (Subfamily Polyommatinae) are generally bright blue on the wings above. The sexes differ, and females may be brown or dark gray. The wings beneath are typically whitish gray with dark markings and distinct hindwing eyespots. The eyes are wrapped around the base of the antennae. The palpi are reduced and close to the head. Adults have a moderately quick and erratic flight, usually low to the ground. At rest, they hold their wings together over the back. Males frequently puddle at damp ground. Most blues are fond of open, disturbed sites with weedy vegetation.

Metalmarks (Subfamily Riodininae) are characterized by metallic flecks of color or even overall metallic-looking wings. They have eyes entirely separate from the antennal bases, and the palpi are quite prominent. Metalmarks reach a tremendous

diversity of colors and patterns in the tropics. Most US species are small rust, gray, or brownish butterflies. They characteristically perch with their wings outstretched and may often land on the underside of leaves, especially if disturbed. Adults have a low, scurrying flight. Several species are of conservation concern.

Hairstreaks (Subfamily Theclinae) tend to be larger than blues. The wings below are often intricately patterned and bear colorful eyespots adjacent to one or two small, distinct, hair-like tails on each hindwing. The adults have a quick, erratic flight and can be a challenge to follow. They regularly visit flowers and hold their wings together over the back while feeding and at rest. Additionally, they have a unique behavior of moving their hindwings up and down when perched. The sexes regularly differ. Hairstreaks can be found in a wide range of habitats. Many species have a single spring generation.

Nymphalidae: Brush-Foots

Brush-foots are the largest and most diverse family of butterflies. In all members, the first pair of legs are significantly reduced and modified into small, brush-like structures, giving the family its name and the appearance of only having four legs.

Emperors (Subfamily Apaturinae) are of medium size and with short, stubby bodies and a robust thorax. Their wings typically have dark markings and small, dark eyespots. The adults are strong and rapid fliers. Males establish territories and perch on tree trunks or overhanging branches. At rest, they hold their wings together over the back. They feed on dung, carrion, rotting fruit, or tree sap and do not visit flowers. Emperors inhabit rich woodlands and rarely venture far into open areas. They are nervous butterflies and difficult to closely approach.

Leafwings (Subfamily Charaxinae) are medium-sized butterflies with irregular wing margins. They are bright tawny orange above, but mottled gray to brown below, and resemble a dead leaf when resting with their wings closed. The adults have a strong, rapid, and erratic flight. They are nervous butterflies and difficult to closely approach. Males establish territories and perch on tree trunks or overhanging branches. Individuals also often land on the ground. They feed on dung, carrion, rotting fruit, or tree sap and do not visit flowers.

Milkweed butterflies (Subfamily Danainae) are large butterflies with boldly marked black-and-orange wings. Their flight is strong and swift with periods of gliding. Adults are strongly attracted to flowers and feed with their wings folded tightly over their backs. Males have noticeable black scent patches in the middle of each hindwing. This subfamily includes the Monarch, which undergoes massive, long-distance migrations.

Longwing butterflies (Subfamily Heliconiinae) are colorful, medium-sized butterflies. They have narrow, elongated wings, slender bodies, long antennae, and large eyes. Their flight tends to be slow and fluttering. The adults readily visit flowers and nectar with their wings open. Most tend to be long-lived. Within the group are fritillaries. They are small- to medium-sized orange and black butterflies of open, sunny habitats. The Great Spangled Fritillary (pg. 295) is a fine example of this group. It, like other members of the genus *Speyeria*, has boldly patterned ventral hindwings with metallic silver spots.

Snouts (Subfamily Libytheinae) are medium-sized, generally drab brown butterflies representing about 10 species worldwide with only one found in the US. They have extremely elongated labial palpi and cryptically colored ventral hindwings. They rest with their wings tightly closed and resemble dead leaves.

Admirals (Subfamily Limenitidinae) are medium- to large-size butterflies with broad, colorful wings. The adults fly with a series of quick wingbeats followed by a brief period of gliding. They are typically associated with immature, secondary-growth woodlands or semiopen shrubby sites. Males perch on sunlit leaves or branches and make periodic exploratory flights. They will feed at flowers as well as upon rotting fruit, dung, carrion, and tree sap.

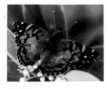

True brush-foots (Subfamily Nymphalinae) are colorful, small- to medium-sized butterflies with no overall common wing shape. Most have stubby, compact bodies and a robust thorax. The adults have a strong, quick flight, usually low to the ground. Most are nervous and often difficult to approach. At rest, they hold their wings together over the back. Many are attracted to flowers, while others feed on dung, carrion, rotting fruit, or tree sap.

Satyrs and **wood-nymphs** (Subfamily Satyrinae) are small- to medium-sized drab brown butterflies. Their wings are marked with dark stripes and prominent eyespots. The adults have a slow, somewhat bobbing flight, usually low to the ground. They inhabit shady woodlands and adjacent open, grassy areas. The

adults rarely visit flowers. They are instead attracted to dung, carrion, rotting fruit, or tree sap. At rest, they hold their wings together over their backs and are generally easy to closely approach. They regularly land on the ground.

Papilionidae: Swallowtails

Swallowtails are easily recognized by their large size and noticeably long hindwing tails. They are generally dark with bold markings. The adults have a swift and powerful flight, usually several meters off the ground, and regularly visit flowers. Most swallowtails continuously flutter their wings while feeding. Males often puddle at damp ground. They generally are found in and along woodland areas and adjacent open sites.

Pieridae: Sulphurs and Whites

Members of this butterfly family are small- to medium-sized butterflies, typically some shade of white or yellow. Many have dark markings. Most species are sexually dimorphic and seasonally variable. The adults have a moderately quick and erratic flight, usually low to the ground. They are fond of flowers and hold their wings together over the back while feeding. Males often puddle at damp ground. *Sulphurs* (Subfamily Coliadinae) and *whites* (Subfamily Pierinae) are common butterflies of open, disturbed sites where their weedy larval host plants abound.

Moth Families

Moths are incredibly diverse. Globally, there are nearly over 120 families of moths and nearly 10 times as many moth species as butterflies. Here are the few moth families included in the book.

Saturniidae: Emperor, Royal, Moon, and Giant Silk Moths. This family contains some of our largest and most charismatic species such as the Luna Moth, Polyphemus Moth, and Cecropia Moth. Adults are mostly nocturnal. They tend to have robust, hairy bodies; large, often colorful wings; ferny antennae; and reduced mouthparts. Seeing one is always a treat!

Sphingidae: Sphinx Moths. Also called Hawk Moths, the adults may be crepuscular, nocturnal, or day-flying. They are large to medium-sized insects with long narrow wings, robust elongated bodies, and a powerful flight. Most have a well-developed proboscis and feed at flowers like a hummingbird. Many of their larvae, commonly called hornworms, have a distinctive horn-like projection off the rear end.

Erebidae: Underwing, Tiger, Tussock, and Allied Moths. Erebidae represents the largest and most diverse family within the Lepidoptera. It includes some familiar groups, including wasp moths, litter moths, and lichen moths. Most are nocturnal. The adults typically rest with their wings folded flat or tent-like over their backs. While most are somewhat drab and cryptic, tiger and wasp moths can be more brightly colored.

Noctuidae: Owlet Moths. Also called Cutworms, the Noctuidae are a large and diverse family of moths. Adults are mostly nocturnal, drab in color, and rest with their wings folded flat or tent-like over their backs. Some species are considered agricultural or forest pests.

OBSERVING BUTTERFLIES AND MOTHS
IN THE FIELD

While butterflies and moths are entertaining and beautiful to watch, correctly identifying them can often be a challenge. But it's generally not as difficult as it might seem. With a little practice and some basic guidelines, you can quickly learn to identify that unknown butterfly.

One of the first and most obvious things to note when you spot a butterfly is its size. You will discover that butterflies generally come in one of three basic dimensions: small, medium, and large. This system may sound ridiculously arbitrary at first, but when you begin to regularly observe several different butterflies together in the field, these categories quickly start to make sense. For a starting point, follow this simple strategy: the next time you see a Monarch Butterfly, pay close attention to its size. You may wish to use your hand as a reference. Most Monarchs have a wingspan close to the length of your palm (about four inches) as measured from the base of your fingers to the start of your wrist. This is considered a large butterfly. From here it's basically a matter of fractions. A medium-sized butterfly by comparison would have a wingspan of generally about half that size (about two inches). Finally, a butterfly would be considered small if it had a wingspan one quarter that of a Monarch (around one inch).

Next, pay close attention to the color and pattern of the wings. This field guide is organized by color, and you can quickly navigate to the appropriate section. First, start by noting the overall ground color. Is it, for example, primarily black, yellow, orange, or white? Then try to identify any major pattern elements such as distinct stripes, bands, or spots.

Depending on the behavior of the butterfly in the wild, keep in mind that the most visible portion of a butterfly may either be the upper surface of the wings (dorsal surface) or the underside (ventral surface). If you have a particularly cooperative subject, you may be able to closely observe both sides. Finally, carefully note the color and position of any major markings. For example, if the butterfly has a wide yellow band on the forewing, is it positioned in the middle of the wing or along the outer edge? Lepidopterists have a detailed vocabulary for wing pattern positions. The illustrations on page 11, of general wing features and wing areas, should help you become familiar with some terminology.

Next, note the shape of the butterfly's wings, particularly the forewings. Are they generally long and narrow, rounded, broad, pointed, or angled? Butterflies such as the Meadow Fritillary have somewhat elongated wings. Others, like the Little Wood-Satyr and Eastern Tailed-Blue, have short, generally rounded wings. Next, do the wings have any unique features? Many swallowtails and hairstreaks have distinct hindwing tails, while Question Marks and Eastern Commas have visibly irregular wing margins. Clues like this can help you quickly narrow the butterfly down to a particular family or distinguish it from a similarly colored species.

The way a butterfly flies may also be useful for identification. While it is generally difficult to easily pick up particular features or color patterns when a butterfly is moving, its flight pattern can often be very distinctive. Carefully follow the butterfly as it flies and watch how it behaves in the air. Is it soaring above your head or scurrying rapidly along the ground? Is it moving fast and erratically or fluttering slowly about? Monarchs, for instance, have a very unique flight pattern: They flap their wings quickly several times, glide for bit, and then quickly flap their wings again. Other butterflies, such as most wood-nymphs and satyrs, have a characteristic low, bobbing flight.

Sometimes you can gain important clues about a butterfly by the way it behaves when feeding. Next time you see a butterfly feeding, watch its wings. Does it hold them tightly closed, spread them wide open, or flutter them? Most swallowtails continuously flutter their wings. This behavior is a quick and reliable diagnostic that can be seen from a fair distance.

Note the habitat in which the butterfly occurs. Is it darting between branches along a shady and moist woodland path? Perched on the top of a grass blade in a saltwater marsh? Bobbing among low grasses in a wet prairie? Fluttering from one flower to the next in a fallow agricultural field?

Many butterflies have strong habitat preferences. Some are restricted to a single particular habitat, while others may occur in a wide range of places.

Sometimes even the date can offer a useful hint. Many hairstreaks are univoltine, meaning they produce just one generation. As a result, the adults occur only during a narrow window of time each spring. Similarly, several butterflies over-winter as adults. They may be active at times when few other species are around.

Butterfly observation and identification are skills, and it takes time and practice to master them. To speed up the learning curve, you may also wish to join a local butterfly club or society (see page 393 for more information). The members can help give advice, accompany you in the field, or share directions to great butterfly watching spots.

DETERMINING A BUTTERFLY'S COLOR

To help make butterfly field identification fun and easy, this guide is organized by color, allowing you to quickly navigate to the appropriate section. In addition, smaller butterflies are always toward the beginning of each section, and the largest are toward the back. Butterflies are not static subjects, so determining their color can be a bit tricky. Several factors such as age, seasonal variation, and complex wing and color patterns may affect your perception of a butterfly's color.

Age

Adult age can influence a butterfly's color. While butterflies don't get wrinkles or gray hairs, they do continue to lose wing scales during their life. This type of normal wing wear, combined with more-significant wing damage, can cause once-vibrant colors or iridescence to fade and pattern elements to become less distinct. As a result, the bright tawny orange wings of a freshly emerged Great Spangled Fritillary may appear dull orange or almost yellowish in an old individual.

Seasonal Variation

Time of year can play a role as well. Some butterflies produce distinct seasonal forms that may vary significantly in color and to a lesser extent in wing shape or overall size. For the Sleepy Orange, the change is dramatic. Individuals produced during the summer are bright butter yellow on the wings below. Winter forms, by contrast, have dark rust-colored ventral hindwings, perfect for blending into a predominantly brown fall and winter landscape. For species that display extensive seasonal variation, the differences are discussed as well.

Complex Wing and Color Patterns

For many butterflies, wing color and pattern can vary tremendously between the dorsal and ventral surface. The wings of a White M Hairstreak are brilliant iridescent blue above and brownish gray below. The bright dorsal coloration is readily visible during flight but concealed at rest when the hairstreak holds its wings firmly closed. As a result, the butterfly may appear either blue or black depending on your perspective and the butterfly's activity.

Most hairstreaks (subfamily Theclinae) and sulphurs (subfamily Coliadinae) typically feed and rest with their wings closed. As a result, very few photographs of the dorsal wing surface of free-flying butterflies in these groups exist. Similarly, most blues (subfamily Polyommatinae) perch and feed with their wings closed or hold them only partially open when basking. Many of these same butterflies are also two-toned (blue on the dorsal surface but whitish to grubby gray below; or orange on the dorsal surface but much yellower below). But because a large number of these butterflies are so small, chances are that you'll notice them first when they fly and reveal their brighter dorsal coloration. Two-toned butterflies such as these have been placed in the color section that reflects the brighter coloration that you're most likely to notice first.

For example, if you're looking in the white section for a small butterfly with lots of bands and spots on the ventral surface but you can't find it, try the blue section. You might be looking at a perched Spring Azure, which is bright blue above but a rather nondescript brownish gray white below. Color can vary slightly even among butterflies of the same species. If you see a butterfly that appears to be tawny colored but you can't find it in the orange section, try the brown section. You might be looking at a Tawny Emperor, which can be perceived as orange or brown, depending on the individual.

Finally, females are generally drabber than males of the same species. They can have less iridescent color, and fewer or darker markings, and they can appear overall darker or paler.

BUTTERFLY Q & A:
What's the difference between a butterfly and a moth?

While there is no one simple answer to this question, butterflies and moths generally differ based on their overall habits and structure. Butterflies are typically active during the day (diurnal), while moths predominantly fly at night (nocturnal). Butterflies possess slender antennae that are clubbed at the end. Those of moths vary from long, narrow filaments to broad, fern-like structures. At rest, butterflies tend to hold their wings together vertically over the back. Moths rest with their wings extended flat out to the sides or folded alongside the body.

Butterflies generally have long, smooth, and slender bodies. The bodies of moths are often robust and hairy. Finally, most butterflies are typically brightly colored, while most moths tend to be dark and somewhat drab.

What can butterflies/moths see?

Butterflies are believed to have very good vision and to see a single color image. Compared to humans, they have an expanded range of sensitivity and are able to distinguish wavelengths of light into the ultraviolet range. Moths, mostly active at night, have adapted to have high-contrast vision.

Do butterflies look the same year-round?

Many butterflies produce distinct seasonal forms that differ markedly in color, size, reproductive activity, and behavior. Good examples within our region, for instance, include the Common Buckeye and Sleepy Orange. The seasonal forms are determined by the environmental cues (temperature, rainfall, day length) that immature stages experience during development. Warm summer temperatures and long days forecast conditions that are highly favorable for continued development and reproduction.

Summer-form individuals are generally lighter in color, short-lived, and reproductively active. As fall approaches, cooler temperatures and shortening day lengths mean future conditions may be unfavorable for continued development and reproduction. Winter-form adults display increased pattern elements, are generally darker, larger, and longer lived, and they survive the winter in a state of reproductive diapause.

Do caterpillars have eyes?

Yes, caterpillars or larvae generally have six pairs of simple eyes called ocelli. They are able to distinguish basic changes in light intensity but are believed to be incapable of forming an image.

How do caterpillars defend themselves?

Caterpillars or larvae are generally plump, slow-moving creatures that represent an inviting meal for many predators. To protect themselves, caterpillars employ a variety of different strategies. Many, like the Monarch or Pipevine Swallowtail, sequester specific chemicals from their host plants that render them highly distasteful or toxic. These caterpillars are generally brightly colored to advertise their unpalatability. Others rely on deception or camouflage to avoid being eaten. White Admiral larvae are mottled green, brown, and cream, a color pattern that helps them resemble a bird dropping. By contrast, larvae of the Northern Pearly-Eye are solid green and extremely well camouflaged against the green leaves of their host.

Some larvae conceal their whereabouts by constructing shelters. American Lady larvae weave leaves and flowerheads together with silk and rest safely inside when not actively feeding. Still others have formidable spines and hairs or produce irritating or foul-smelling chemicals to deter persistent predators. For more about caterpillars, see page 388.

Do butterfly caterpillars make silk?

Yes, butterfly larvae produce silk. While they don't typically spin an elaborate cocoon around their pupa like moths, they use silk for a variety of purposes, including the construction of shelters, anchoring or attaching their chrysalid, and to gain secure footing on leaves and branches.

What happens when the scales of a butterfly or moth rub off?

Contrary to superstition, if you touch a moth/butterfly's wing and remove scales in the process it is still capable of flying. In fact, a butterfly typically continuously loses scales during its life from normal wing wear. Scales serve a variety of purposes, from thermoregulation and camouflage to pheromone dispersal and species or sex recognition, but they're not critical for flight. Once gone, the scales are permanently lost and will not grow back.

Why do butterflies gather at mud puddles?

Adult butterflies are often attracted to damp or moist ground and may congregate at such areas in large numbers. In most cases, these groupings, or "puddle clubs," are made up entirely of males. They drink from the moisture to gain water and salts (sodium ions) that happen to come into solution. This behavior helps males replenish the sodium ions lost when they transfer a packet of sperm and accessory-gland secretions to the female during copulation. The transferred nutrients have been shown to play a significant role in egg production and, thus, female reproductive output.

How long do butterflies live?

In general, most butterflies are extremely short-lived and survive in the wild for an average of about two weeks. There are, of course, numerous exceptions to this rule. The Mourning Cloak is a perfect example: Adults may survive for four to six months. Still others, particularly species that migrate long distances and/or overwinter as adults, are capable of surviving for extended periods of time.

Where do butterflies go at night? Where do they go during a rainstorm?

In the evening or during periods of inclement weather, most butterflies seek shelter under the leaves of growing plants or among vegetation.

Do all butterflies visit flowers?

All butterflies are fluid feeders. While a large percentage of them rely on sugar-rich nectar as the primary energy source for flight, reproduction, and general maintenance, many species also feed on, or exclusively utilize, the liquids and dissolved nutrients produced by other food resources such as dung, carrion, rotting fruit or vegetation, sap, and bird droppings.

Do butterflies and moths grow?

No. An adult butterfly or moth is fully grown upon emergence from its chrysalis/cocoon.

How do caterpillars grow?

A caterpillar's job in life is to eat and grow. But larvae, like all other insects, have an external skeleton. Therefore, in order to increase in size, they must shed their skin, or molt, several times during development. Essentially, their skin is like a trash bag. It is packed full of food until there is no more room. Once full, it is discarded for a larger, baggier one underneath, and the process continues.

What eats butterflies and moths?

Butterflies and moths face an uphill battle for survival. Out of every 100 eggs produced by a female butterfly, only about 1 percent survive to become an adult. And as an adult, the odds don't get much better. Various birds, small mammals, lizards, frogs, toads, spiders, and other insects all prey on butterflies and moths.

Whats the difference between a chrysalis and a cocoon?

Once fully grown, both moth and butterfly caterpillars molt a final time to form a pupa. Most moths surround their pupae with a constructed silken case called a cocoon. By contrast, a butterfly pupa, frequently termed a chrysalis, is generally naked. In most cases, butterfly chrysalids are attached to a leaf, twig, or other surface with silk. In some instances, they may be unattached or surrounded by a loose silken cocoon.

Are all butterfly scales the same?

No. The scales on a butterfly's wings and body come in a variety of different sizes and shapes. Some may be extremely elongated and resemble hairs, while others are highly modified for the release of pheromones during courtship. Those responsible for making up wing color and pattern are generally wide and flat. They are attached at the base and overlap like shingles on a roof. The colors we see are the result of either pigments contained in the scales or the diffraction of light caused by scale structure. Iridescent colors such as blue, green, purple, and silver usually result from scale structure. While pigmented scales are the norm, many species have a combination of both types on their wings.

Why do butterflies often sit in the bright sun?

Unlike mammals and birds, butterflies are poikilothermic or cold-blooded organisms. They do not have an internal mechanism to regulate body temperature, so they must instead rely on a variety of behaviors for thermoregulation. Basking in the warm sunlight is one of the most obvious method and is typically witnessed on cool days or during the morning hours. The butterfly positions its wings at an appropriate angle to capture and transport the sun's heat to the thoracic flight muscles, thereby slowly raising the body temperature to the level needed for flight.

Why are butterflies and moths important?

Butterflies and moths play a number of important roles in the environment. Like bees or wasps, they are pollinators helping to facilitate plant reproduction. They also provide a wealth of food resources for other organisms. Birds, lizards, frogs, spiders, small mammals, and various predacious insects may all feed on butterflies or moths in one life stage or another. Additionally, as butterflies and other insects are able to produce a large number of generations in a relatively short time, they tend to react to changes in the environment much more quickly than birds or mammals. Therefore, they are indicator species that help act like a barometer of ecological health. Due to their tremendous nationwide popularity, butterflies often act as flagship species helping to rally support for various conservation efforts such as habitat protection. Finally, butterflies and moths are colorful and graceful creatures that help promote exploration of the outdoors.

Compare: describes differences among similar-looking species
Comments: interesting notes about each species

Common Name
Scientific Name

Family/Subfamily: the family and subfamily the butterfly or moth belongs to (see pages 13–20 for descriptions)

Wingspan: the average wingspan for each species, from one wingtip to the other

Above: description of the upper, or dorsal, surface of wings

Below: description of the lower, or ventral, surface of wings

Sexes: differences in appearance between male and female

Egg: description of eggs and where they are deposited

Larva: description of the butterfly or moth's larva, or caterpillar

Larval Host Plants: plants that eggs and larvae are likely to be found on

Habitat: where you're likely to find the butterflies or moths

Broods: the number of broods, or generations, hatched in the span of a year

Abundance: how often you're likely to encounter each species

Range: the geographic range of each species

Compare: unique

Comments: This spectacularly colored species is truly a must-see butterfly. Unfortunately, like many other wetland specialists, it has declined in many areas due to habitat loss or alteration. Populations tend to be localized but at times are fairly abundant. The Baltimore Checkerspot has a somewhat unusual life history. Females primarily lay eggs on White Turtlehead. Upon hatching, the larvae construct a communal web and feed gregariously until late summer. In fall, the partially grown larvae overwinter in groups at the base of the plant. The larvae resume feeding in spring but may utilize a variety of plant species to complete development.

Baltimore Checkerspot
Euphydryas phaeton

Family/Subfamily: Brush-Footed Butterflies (Nymphalidae)/ True Brush-Foots (Nymphalinae)

Wingspan: 1.75–2.4" (4.4–6.1 cm)

Above: black with prominent orange spots along the outer margin of the wings and several rows of smaller white spots; forewing cell has large-to-reduced orange spots; forewing is somewhat elongated

Below: marked as above with additional orange basal spots on both wings

Sexes: similar

Egg: small, yellow, laid in large clusters of several hundred on the underside of host leaves; eggs turn orange before they hatch

Larva: tawny orange with black transverse stripes and several rows of black, branched spines; front and rear segments are all black

Larval Host Plants: White Turtlehead (*Chelone glabra*) is the primary host; secondary hosts include plantain (*Plantago* spp.), Swamp Lousewort (*Pedicularis lanceolata*), beardtongue (*Penstemon* spp.), false foxglove (*Agalinis* spp.), and others

Habitat: wet meadows, marshes, fens, bogs, stream margins, and moist fields

Broods: one generation; larvae overwinter

Abundance: rare to occasional; can be locally common

Range: throughout much of the region; absent westward in the Dakotas and Nebraska

ventral

Compare: unique

Comments: Widespread and common throughout the US and southern Canada, the Red Admiral is easily distinguished from all other species by its bold, reddish dorsal forewing band. A butterfly of rich woodlands and other moist sites, it nonetheless readily explores adjacent habitats in search of nectar and can be a frequent garden visitor. It occasionally experiences tremendous population outbreaks. The species is typically unable to survive the winter in northern locations and annually migrates south in the fall to overwinter. Individuals then quickly recolonize the central and northern states in spring.

Red Admiral
Vanessa atalanta

Family/Subfamily: Brush-Footed Butterflies (Nymphalidae)/ True Brush-Foots (Nymphalinae)

Wingspan: 1.75–2.5" (4.4–6.4 cm)

Above: dark brownish black with broad, reddish-orange hindwing border and prominent, reddish-orange median forewing band; forewing has several white spots near the squared-off apex

Below: forewing as above with some blue scaling and muted colors; hindwing is ornately mottled with dark brown, blue, and cream in a bark-like pattern

Sexes: similar

Egg: small, green, singly laid on host leaves

Larva: variable; pinkish gray to charcoal with lateral row of cream crescent-shaped spots and numerous branched spines; constructs individual leaf shelters by folding one or more leaves together with silk

Larval Host Plants: Smallspike False Nettle (*Boehmeria cylindrica*), Canada Wood Nettle (*Laportea canadensis*), Stinging Nettle (*Urtica dioica*), and Pennsylvania Pellitory (*Parietaria pensylvanica*)

Habitat: moist woodlands, forest margins, roadside ditches, wetland margins, parks, wet meadows, yards, and gardens

Broods: two or more generations; adults overwinter

Abundance: occasional to common; locally abundant

Range: throughout

Compare: Spicebush Swallowtail (pg. 49) is larger and has greenish-blue submarginal spots; Pipevine Swallowtail (pg. 41) lacks yellow ventral spots and has only one row of orange spots on the ventral hindwing

Comments: Wide-ranging and generally common, the Black Swallowtail is one of our most frequently encountered garden butterflies. Its plump, green, larvae often referred to as "parsley worms," feed on many cultivated herbs and may become minor pests in vegetable gardens. It is as at home in undisturbed wetlands and rural meadows as it is in suburban yards and urban parks. Males have a strong, quick flight and actively patrol open areas for females. Both sexes are exceedingly fond of flowers and are readily drawn into landscapes with abundant blooms. Females mimic the toxic Pipevine Swallowtail for protection from predators.

Black Swallowtail

Papilio polyxenes

Family/Subfamily: Swallowtails (Papilionidae)/
Swallowtails (Papilioninae)

Wingspan: 2.5–4.2" (6.4–10.7 cm)

Above: wings are black; male has a broad, postmedian yellow
spot band and row of marginal yellow spots; female is mostly
black with increased blue hindwing scaling and marginal
yellow spots; postmedian yellow spot band is reduced; both
sexes have a red hindwing eyespot with a central black pupil
adjacent to a single tail; abdomen is black with longitudinal
rows of yellow spots

Below: hindwing has blue scaling between yellow-tinged orange
postmedian and marginal spots

Sexes: dissimilar; female has reduced yellow postmedian spot
band and increased blue hindwing scaling

Egg: round, pale yellow, laid singly host leaves or flowers

Larva: green with black transverse bands containing yellow-
orange spots

Larval Host Plants: wild and cultivated members of the carrot
family (Apiaceae), including angelica (*Angelica* spp.), Queen
Anne's Lace (*Daucus carota*), meadowparsnip (*Thaspium*
spp.), and Spotted Water Hemlock (*Cicuta maculata*), as well
as dill, fennel, and parsley

Habitat: forest margins, roadsides, old fields, prairie, wet meadows, fallow agricultural lands, utility corridors, parks, yards,
and gardens

Broods: two to three generations; pupae overwinter

Abundance: occasional to abundant

Range: generally throughout; less common in northwest portions

ventral

Compare: Spicebush Swallowtail (pg. 49) is larger with prominent crescent-shaped submarginal spots; Red-Spotted Purple
(pg. 43) lacks hindwing tails; female Black Swallowtail (pg. 39)
is larger with an orange hindwing spot; dark-form female
Eastern Tiger Swallowtail (pg. 337) is much larger and often
has faint black stripes, especially on the ventral surface.

Comments: Our smallest black-colored swallowtail, it is most
common throughout the southeastern half of the region. It
is absent, rare, or locally sporadic farther north and west,
temporarily colonizing available planted Pipevines. Farther
south, one or more native Pipevine species naturally occur.
The Pipevine Swallowtail's fleshy larvae sequester toxins from
their host plants, rendering them and the resulting adults
highly distasteful to certain predators. The butterfly's bold
orange and black ventral hindwing pattern visibly advertise
this unpalatability.

Pipevine Swallowtail
Battus philenor

Family/Subfamily: Swallowtails (Papilionidae)/
Swallowtails (Papilioninae)

Wingspan: 2.75–4.0" (7.0–10.2 cm)

Above: overall black; males have iridescent, greenish-blue scaling on hindwings; female is duller black with a single row of white submarginal spots

Below: hindwings have broad, iridescent-blue scaling on outer half with a row of prominent orange spots

Sexes: dissimilar; female is dull black with more prominent row of white spots

Egg: brownish orange, round, laid singly or in small clusters on host

Larva: velvety black with orange spots and numerous fleshy tubercles; superficially resembles a centipede

Larval Host Plants: various pipevines (*Aristolochia* spp.), including Virginia Snakeroot (*Aristolochia serpentaria*), Woolly Dutchman's Pipe (*A. tomentosa*), and Pipevine (*A. macrophylla*)

Habitat: open woodlands; forest margins; and adjacent open areas, including clearings, stream margins, roadsides, yards, and gardens

Broods: two; pupae overwinter

Abundance: rare to common

Range: primarily southern portions of the region; absent from North and South Dakota; uncommon in Nebraska; uncommon stray or temporary breeding colonist northward; unlikely to survive winters in more-northern portions of the range

ventral

Compare: White Admiral (pg. 45) has a broad white postmedian band across the wings

Comments: The Red-Spotted Purple is a large, predominantly black butterfly named for the brilliant, iridescent blue sheen (especially vibrant in fresh individuals) and the bold, deep-orange (not red) spots on the wings below. It is one of four butterflies in the region that mimic the toxic Pipevine Swallowtail (pg. 41) to help protect them from predation. While widespread and common, the butterfly is seldom seen in large numbers. Adults rarely visit flowers but instead feed on animal dung, urine, rotting fruit, and tree sap. It readily hybridizes with the White Admiral across a broad zone from the eastern Dakotas to northern Ohio.

Red-Spotted Purple
Limenitis arthemis astyanax

Family/Subfamily: Brush-Footed Butterflies (Nymphalidae)/ Admirals (Limenitidinae)

Wingspan: 3.0–3.5" (7.6–9.5 cm)

Above: velvety bluish black with an overall iridescent-blue sheen; has prominent iridescent-blue scaling on the outer half of the hindwing; forewing often has some orange and white spots near the apex

Below: brownish black with a row of iridescent-blue marginal spots; a submarginal row of orange spots and orange basal spots; forewing often has a few small white spots located near the apex

Sexes: similar

Egg: gray green, laid singly on the tips of host leaves

Larva: variable; mottled olive green, brown, and cream with two long, knobby horns off the thorax; some larvae are browner; resembles a bird dropping. Young larvae eat the tip of the leaf to the midvein and rest on the end of the vein when not actively feeding.

Larval Host Plants: Black Cherry (*Prunus serotina*), Deerberry (*Vaccinium stamineum*), and willow (*Salix* spp.); also aspen, cottonwood, and poplar (*Populus* spp.)

Habitat: deciduous woodlands, margins, trails, clearings, forested roadsides, and adjacent open areas; forested parks, yards, and neighborhoods

Broods: two generations; larvae overwinter

Abundance: occasional to common

Range: throughout the southern two-thirds of the region; occasionally farther north; absent or limited in western portions

ventral

Compare: Red-Spotted Purple (pg. 43) lacks the broad, white postmedian bands across the wings

Comments: This distinctively stunning butterfly of northern forests essentially replaces the closely related Red-Spotted Purple throughout much of the Upper Midwest, Northeast, and southeastern Canada. The two often hybridize in areas where their ranges overlap. Numerous intergradations may be found across this broad "hybrid zone." Adults have a strong, gliding flight and are often quite wary. Males regularly perch on sunlit leaves for passing females and make periodic exploratory flights. Both sexes will visit flowers but prefer rotting fruit and animal dung. Fresh individuals are incredibly electric-looking.

White Admiral
Limenitis arthemis arthemis

Family/Subfamily: Brush-Footed Butterflies (Nymphalidae)/ Admirals (Limenitidinae)

Wingspan: 3.0–3.75" (7.6–8.9 cm)

Above: velvety bluish black with a broad, white postmedian band across both wings; forewing has a few white apical spots; hindwing has a submarginal row of orange spots and iridescent-blue dashes along the margin

Below: brownish black with a broad, white postmedian band and a submarginal row of reddish-orange spots across both wings; forewing has a few white apical spots; hindwings has a few reddish-orange spots near the base

Sexes: similar

Egg: gray green, laid singly on the tips of host leaves

Larva: mottled olive green, brown, and cream with two long, knobby horns off the thorax; resembles a bird dropping. Young larvae eat the tip of the leaf to the midvein and rest on the end of the vein when not actively feeding.

Larval Host Plants: birch (*Betula* spp.) and willow (*Salix* spp.) as well as aspen, cottonwood, and poplar (*Populus* spp.)

Habitat: woodland margins, trails, clearings, forested roadsides, and adjacent open areas

Broods: two generations; larvae overwinter

Abundance: occasional to common

Range: throughout the northern third of the region; occasionally farther south

Compare: unique

Comments: Despite its morbid name, the Mourning Cloak is richly beautiful and often the first harbinger of spring, with some overwintering individuals coming out of hibernation when there is still some snow on the ground. It is also one of our longest-lived species, with some individuals surviving nearly 11 months. Adult butterflies first eclose (complete metamorphosis) in early summer, estivate (hibernate) until fall, become active again to feed, and build fat reserves before seeking protected sites to overwinter. In early spring, these adults become active again, mate, and lay eggs. The showy larvae are gregarious and feed together in communal silken webs on host trees.

Mourning Cloak
Nymphalis antiopa

Family/Subfamily: Brush-Footed Butterflies (Nymphalidae)/ True Brush-Foots (Nymphalinae)

Wingspan: 3.0–4.0" (7.6–10.2 cm)

Above: velvety reddish brown to chocolate brown with a broad, irregular yellow wing border and submarginal row of blue spots; forewing apex is squared-off and hooked; hindwing has a short, stubby tail

Below: silky black with a broad, pale wing border; heavily striated and bark-like appearance

Sexes: similar

Egg: small, barrel-shaped, yellow brown but darkens considerably before hatching; laid in large clusters on host leaves or twigs

Larva: black with a dorsal row of crimson patches; fine white speckling, and several rows of black, branched spines

Larval Host Plants: various trees, including hackberry (*Celtis* spp.), elm (*Ulmus* spp.), willow (*Salix* spp.), and birch (*Betula* spp.); also poplar, aspen, and cottonwood (*Populus* spp.)

Habitat: rich, deciduous woodlands; margins and adjacent open areas; wetlands and watercourse margins; riparian woodlands; parks, yards, and neighborhoods

Broods: one generation; adults overwinter

Abundance: occasional to common

Range: throughout, although less common to absent in far northwest portions of the region

ventral

Compare: Pipevine Swallowtail (pg. 41), female Black Swallowtail (pg. 39), and dark-form female Eastern Tiger Swallowtail (pg. 337) all lack greenish-blue marginal spots

Comments: The Spicebush Swallowtail is mostly common in eastern and southern portions of the region. It is yet another butterfly that mimics the toxic Pipevine Swallowtail. Adults have a swift flight but are avid flower visitors. The charismatic larvae display very realistic-looking false eyes that resemble the head of a small snake or lizard. They construct individual leaf shelters on their host and rest safely inside when they are not feeding. Males actively visit moist soil, animal urine, and dung.

Spicebush Swallowtail

Papilio troilus

Family/Subfamily: Swallowtails (Papilionidae)/
   Swallowtails (Papilioninae)

Wingspan: 3.5–4.75" (8.9–12.1 cm)

Above: black with marginal row of large, pale greenish-blue
   spots; hindwings have greenish-blue scaling, an orange
   eyespot, and a single hindwing tail

Below: black with postmedian band of blue scaling bordered
   by row of yellow-orange spots; abdomen is black with row
   of light spots along the side

Sexes: similar; female has duller dorsal hindwing scaling

Egg: cream, round, laid singly on the underside of host leaves
   or budding branches

Larva: green above, reddish below with yellow side stripe
   and row of small blue spots; enlarged thorax with two
   large false eyes

Larval Host Plants: Sassafras (*Sassafras albidum*) and Northern
   Spicebush (*Lindera benzoin*)

Habitat: deciduous woodlands; mixed forests; and adjacent
   margins, clearings, pastures, and gardens

Broods: two generations; pupae overwinter

Abundance: rare to common

Range: primarily lower Michigan southwest through Missouri;
   rare in northern and western portions

Ventral

Compare: Summer Azure (pg. 59) lacks hindwing orange-capped black spots at tail; Western Tailed-Blue (pg. 57) has smaller, less distinct ventral markings, favors more-open forest and shrubby habitat, and is found only in far northern portions of the region

Comments: Widespread and common throughout most of the Midwest and the eastern US, this small species is arguably our most commonly encountered blue. While it is named for the distinctive hair-like hindwing tail, do not rely solely on this feature for identification. The tails are fragile and often lost from normal wing wear or an encounter with a predator. Adults have a weak, dancing flight. Both sexes are very fond of flowers and may be attracted to gardens. Males often gather in small puddle clubs at damp gravel or soil. The Eastern Tailed-Blue typically feeds with its wings closed but perches on low vegetation with its wings partially open.

Eastern Tailed-Blue
Cupido comyntas

Family/Subfamily: Gossamer Wings (Lycaenidae)/
Blues (Polyommatinae)

Wingspan: 0.75–1.0" (1.9–2.5 cm)

Above: male is blue with narrow brown wing border; female
is brownish gray; both sexes have one or two small, orange-
capped black spots above single hindwing tail

Below: silvery gray with numerous dark spots and bands; hindwing has two small, orange-capped black spots near the tail

Sexes: dissimilar; male is blue while female is brownish gray

Egg: pale green, flattened, disc-shaped, laid singly on host
flowers, buds, or young leaves

Larva: slug-like, variable, green to reddish with dark dorsal
stripe and light lateral stripe

Larval Host Plants: various pea family (Fabaceae) plants, including clover (*Trifolium* spp.), vetch (*Vicia* spp.), beggarweed
(*Desmodium* spp.), lespedeza (*Lespedeza* spp.), and sweet
clover (*Melilotus* spp.)

Habitat: open, disturbed sites, including roadsides, old fields,
meadows, easements, and pastures; also prairies, yards,
and home gardens

Broods: multiple generations; larvae overwinter

Abundance: occasional to common

Range: throughout

Reakirt's Blue
Echinargus isola

Family/Subfamily: Gossamer Wings (Lycaenidae)/
Blues (Polyommatinae)

Wingspan: 0.75–1.0" (1.9–2.8 cm)

Habitat: open habitat; prairies to disturbed sites

Range: primarily western half; rare to occasional

Sexes: dissimilar; female is brown dorsally with less blue scaling

Larva: slug-like, green to pinkish red with pale lateral stripe and oblique dashes

Above: male is light blue with narrow, grayish-brown borders; female is primarily grayish brown with blue scaling limited to the wing bases; both sexes have a small but prominent black spot along the outer margin

Below: light gray with numerous white bands; forewing with distinct postmedian row of white-outlined round black spots

Compare: unique

Comments: In our region, Reakirt's Blue is mostly reported from Minnesota and Wisconsin southward. It is unable to survive the harsh winter conditions in the Midwest.

Marine Blue

Leptotes marina

Family/Subfamily: Gossamer Wings (Lycaenidae)/
Blues (Polyommatinae)

Wingspan: 0.75–1.1" (1.9–2.8 cm)

Habitat: open areas, including fields, gardens, and disturbed sites

Range: variable; rare, vagrant

Sexes: dissimilar; female is brown dorsally with less blue scaling

Larva: slug-like, green with a darker green dorsal stripe and
pale oblique dashes

Above: male is light metallic blue with violet cast and narrow
dark borders; female is brown with blue scaling limited to
wing bases and some white extending outward; both sexes
have a small black spot along outer hindwing margin

Below: brown gray with white bands; hindwing has two small,
orange-capped black spots with blue highlights along outer
hindwing margin

Compare: unique

Comments: The Marine Blue is another Southwest resident that
wanders north and east. It is considered a stray in our region.

Compare: Summer Azure (pg. 59) is typically larger and lighter beneath with reduced dark markings and scaling; Northern Azure (pg. 61) is very similar-looking but found primarily across the northern third of the region.

Comments: The Spring Azure is one of our most abundant and noticeable early-season species across much of the region. It is often spotted before many colorful spring trees and shrubs are in bloom. The mottled larvae blend in remarkably well to the host flowers on which they feed. Adults have a moderately slow flight and erratically scurry at low to canopy height over the surface of vegetation. They seek nectar at a variety of flowers, including those of their hosts, and often congregate at damp ground. Adults rest and feed with wings closed, but the violet blue of their wings above is visible mostly in flight or when basking.

Spring Azure
Celastrina ladon

Family/Subfamily: Gossamer Wings (Lycaenidae)/
Blues (Polyommatinae)

Wingspan: 0.75–1.25" (2.0–3.2 cm)

Above: male is pale violet blue with narrow, often faint dark
border; female is light blue, often with increased white
scaling and broad, dark forewing border and narrow
hindwing border

Below: somewhat variable; dusky gray with black spots and dark
chevrons and marks along wing margins

Sexes: dissimilar; female is paler blue and has broader dark
wing borders

Egg: pale green, flattened, disc-shaped, laid singly on host
flower buds

Larva: slug-like, variable, green to greenish pink with pale
oblique marks

Larval Host Plants: flowers of various trees and shrubs, including
New Jersey Tea (*Ceanothus americana*), dogwood (*Cornus*
spp.), viburnum (*Viburnum* spp.), Black Cherry (*Prunus
serotina*), and meadowsweet (*Spirea* spp.)

Habitat: open, deciduous forests, forest edges, clearings and
nearby shrubby areas, wooded swamps, parks, and yards

Broods: single generation; pupae overwinter

Abundance: occasional to common

Range: southern two-thirds of the region

Dusky Azure
Celastrina nigra

Family/Subfamily: Gossamer Wings (Lycaenidae)/
Blues (Polyommatinae)

Wingspan: 0.75–1.25" (1.9–3.2 cm)

Habitat: moist, rich, shaded woodlands

Range: found only in southern Ohio; rare to uncommon; localized

Sexes: dissimilar; female is gray blue with wide forewing borders

Egg: pale blue green, flattened, disc-shaped, laid singly on host
flower buds, new shoots, or new leaves

Larva: slug-like, yellow green; single brood; pupae overwinter

Above: male is uniform dark charcoal gray; female is pale gray
blue with extensive dark wing borders

Below: light gray with small black spots; hindwing has pale but
prominent dark zigzag band along the outer margin, enclosing a row of dark spots

Compare: Spring Azure (pg. 55)

Comments: The Dusky Azure is distinguished by its dark, gray-
infused dorsal wings.

Western Tailed-Blue
Cupido amyntula

Family/Subfamily: Gossamer Wings (Lycaenidae)/
Blues (Polyommatinae)

Wingspan: 0.8–1.1" (2.0–2.8 cm)

Habitat: forest edges, clearings, and nearby shrubby areas

Range: far northern and western parts of the region; rare

Sexes: dissimilar; male is blue while female is brownish gray

Larva: slug-like, green with dark dorsal stripe and light lateral
stripe; single generation; larvae overwinter

Above: male is blue with narrow brown wing border; female is
brownish gray with faint blue scaling at wing bases; female
often has small orange-capped black spot(s) above single
hindwing tail

Below: silvery white with numerous, often faint, small dark spots
and bands; hindwing has one or two small orange-capped
black spots near the tail

Compare: Eastern Tailed-Blue (pg. 51)

Comments: The Western Tailed-Blue becomes scarcer and more
localized eastward. It is generally uncommon.

Compare: Spring Azure (pg. 55) and Northern Azure (pg. 61) are duskier gray and more heavily marked ventrally; Eastern Tailed-Blue (pg. 51) has small, orange-capped black spots near single hindwing tail

Comments: The Summer Azure is a widespread and common species throughout most of the Midwest. Now considered a separate species, it was previously considered a lighter, later-generation form of the early-season Spring Azure. Adults are primarily found in and near woodlands but can also be encountered in many suburban yards and gardens. They have a moderately slow, dancing flight and often fly high among the branches of trees and larger shrubs. Males often congregate at damp earth, sometimes in sizable numbers.

Summer Azure

Celastrina neglecta

Family/Subfamily: Gossamer Wings (Lycaenidae)/
Blues (Polyommatinae)

Wingspan: 0.8–1.25" (2.0–3.2 cm)

Above: male is light blue with narrow, often faint dark border;
female is light blue with heavy white scaling and broad, dark
forewing borders

Below: chalky white with small dark spots and bands

Sexes: dissimilar; female has increased dorsal white scaling
and broad forewing borders

Egg: pale green, flattened, disc-shaped, laid singly on host
flower buds

Larva: slug-like, variable; green to greenish pink with pale
oblique marks

Larval Host Plants: flowers of various trees and shrubs, including New Jersey Tea (*Ceanothus americanus*), meadowsweet
(*Spiraea* spp.), dogwood (*Cornus* spp.), sumac (*Rhus* spp.),
and viburnum (*Viburnum* spp.)

Habitat: open deciduous woodlands, forest margins and trails,
stream corridors, roadsides, easements, wooded swamps,
and gardens

Broods: two or more generations; pupae overwinter

Abundance: occasional to common

Range: throughout most of the region

Compare: Spring Azure (pg. 55) is very similar-looking but found primarily across the southern two-thirds of the region and lacks the occasional dark scaling in the central portion of the hindwing

Comments: The Northern Azure is primarily a boreal species that was once considered a subspecies of the Spring Azure. This diminutive, early-season species is highly variable, and there remains some uncertainty regarding the agreed-upon taxonomy. Both species are very similar-looking and may not be reliably separated in the field, especially for those without the central ventral hindwing markings. Nonetheless, adults can be quite common in northern portions of the region.

Northern Azure
Celastrina lucia

Family/Subfamily: Gossamer Wings (Lycaenidae)/
  Blues (Polyommatinae)

Wingspan: 0.85–1.35" (2.16–3.4 cm)

Above: male is pale dusty blue with a narrow, often faint dark
  border; female is light blue, often with increased white
  scaling and broad, dark forewing border and narrow
  hindwing border

Below: somewhat variable; dusky gray with black spots and dark
  chevrons and marks along wing margins; hindwing often has
  central dark scaling

Sexes: dissimilar; female is paler blue with broader dark
  wing borders

Egg: pale green, flattened, disc-shaped, laid singly on host
  flower buds

Larva: slug-like, variable; green to cream-brown to pinkish with
  pale oblique marks.

Larval Host Plants: primarily blueberry (*Vaccinium* spp.)

Habitat: mixed and coniferous forests, woodland margins and
  openings, bogs, and adjacent shrubby areas

Broods: single generation; pupae overwinter

Abundance: occasional to common

Range: northern third of the region

Northern Blue
Plebejus idas nabokovi

Family/Subfamily: Gossamer Wings (Lycaenidae)/ Blues (Polyommatinae)

Wingspan: 0.85–1.20" (2.2–3.0 cm)

Habitat: mixed or pine forests and rocky outcroppings

Range: known only in northern Minnesota, Wisconsin, and Michigan; rare to uncommon; localized

Sexes: dissimilar; female is brown with less blue scaling

Larva: slug-like, light green with a dark-green dorsal stripe and pale side stripe; often tended by ants; single generation

Above: male is bright blue to violet blue with narrow black wing borders and a white wing fringe; hindwing with submarginal row of orange-capped black spots

Below: light gray with numerous white-rimmed black spots and submarginal row of black and orange-capped bluish spots, which are most prominent on the hindwing

Compare: Karner Blue (pg. 68)

Comments: Listed as a threatened or endangered species in several states.

Greenish Blue
Icaricia saepiolus

Family/Subfamily: Gossamer Wings (Lycaenidae)/
Blues (Polyommatinae)

Wingspan: 1.0–1.25" (2.5–3.2 cm)

Habitat: woodland openings and adjacent clearings, moist
meadows, bog margins, and fields and roadsides

Range: extreme northern and western portions of the range;
rare to occasional; localized

Sexes: dissimilar; female is brown dorsally with less blue scaling

Larva: slug-like, green to reddish brown; single generation

Above: male is light metallic blue to greenish blue with a narrow, dark wing border and white fringe; female is brown with
blue scaling limited to wing bases and submarginal row of
faint, orange-capped black spots; forewing in both sexes has
narrow black cell-end bar

Below: whitish gray with many small, white-rimmed black spots

Compare: Northern Blue (pg. 62) and Silvery Blue (pg. 67)

Comments: Named for its iridescent greenish-blue dorsal wings.
Although highly localized in occurrence, it can be common.

Compare: Karner Blue (pg. 68) is restricted to oak savanna and pine barren habitats with lupine; female lacks the submarginal row of orange spots on the dorsal and ventral forewing; range does not overlap

Comments: Common and widespread throughout the western United States and southern Canada, the Melissa Blue extends eastward into Minnesota and Iowa. It is superficially similar to the much less common, range-restricted, and federally endangered Karner Blue, to which it is closely related. In fact, until recently, the Karner Blue was considered an eastern subspecies of the Melissa Blue. A showy little butterfly, Melissa Blues are avid flower visitors, and the males often congregate at moist soil.

Melissa Blue

Plebejus melissa

Family/Subfamily: Gossamer Wings (Lycaenidae)/
Blues (Polyommatinae)

Wingspan: 0.9–1.35" (2.3–3.4 cm)

Above: male is bright blue with narrow black border; female
is gray brown with blue scaling limited to wing bases and a
continuous submarginal row of orange spots on both wings
(appears almost like a continuous band)

Below: whitish gray with numerous small, white-rimmed
black spots and a continuous submarginal row of black-
and-orange-capped spots on both wings

Sexes: dissimilar; female is gray brown dorsally with reduced
blue scaling and dorsal row of orange spots on both wings

Egg: pale blue green, flattened, disc-shaped, laid singly on or
near the host

Larva: slug like, light green with darker green dorsal stripe and
a pale side stripe; larvae are tended to by ants

Larval Host Plants: various pea family plants such as milkvetch
(*Astragalus* spp.), trefoil (*Lotus* spp.), locoweed (*Oxytropis*
spp.), Alfalfa (*Medicago sativa*), and lupine (*Lupinus* spp.)

Habitat: prairies and a variety of open, disturbed sites,
including old fields, fallow agricultural lands, weedy sites,
and alfalfa fields

Broods: three generations; eggs overwinter

Abundance: rare to common

Range: western portions of the region

Compare: Northern Blue (pg. 62) has a row of black-capped orange and blue submarginal spots on the ventral hindwing

Comments: Although fairly dull below, this lovely early-season species flashes brilliant metallic blue in flight or when basking with its wings open. Although widespread, the Silvery Blue tends to be fairly local in occurrence but can often be fairly numerous when encountered. Adults have a quick and often direct flight but frequently stop to nectar at small spring flowers or perch on low vegetation. Males often gather at damp ground. The Silvery Blue is considered vulnerable or imperiled in several eastern states.

Silvery Blue

Glaucopsyche lygdamus

Family/Subfamily: Gossamer Wings (Lycaenidae)/
Blues (Polyommatinae)

Wingspan: 1.0–1.25" (2.5–3.2 cm)

Above: male is a uniform metallic, bright silvery blue with
narrow black wing borders; female is somewhat duller
with broader dark wing borders

Below: light brownish gray with prominent row of white-rimmed,
rounded black spots; spot size is somewhat variable (often
larger in southern portions of the range)

Sexes: dissimilar; female is a duller blue with broader dark
wing borders

Egg: pale blue green, flattened, disc-shaped, laid singly on host
flower buds, new shoots, or new leaves

Larva: slug-like, variable, purplish to gray green with a dark
dorsal stripe and pale white oblique dashes

Larval Host Plants: various pea family plants, including Carolina
Vetch (*Vicia caroliniana*)

Habitat: open woodlands, forested roadsides, utility easements,
ridges and glades, and adjacent meadows and fields

Broods: single generation; pupae overwinter

Abundance: rare to occasional; localized

Range: scattered; more common in northern half

ventral

Karner Blue
Plebejus melissa samuelis

Family/Subfamily: Gossamer Wings (Lycaenidae)/ Blues (Polyommatinae)

Wingspan: 1.0–1.35" (2.5–3.4 cm)

Habitat: oak savannas, pine barrens, utility easements

Range: the Great Lakes states; rare to common; localized

Sexes: dissimilar; female is gray brown with reduced blue scaling and row of orange-capped black spots

Larva: slug-like, light green with darker green dorsal stripe and a pale side stripe; feeds on wild lupine (*Lupinus perennis*)

Above: male is bright blue with narrow black border

Below: whitish gray with numerous small, white-rimmed black spots and submarginal row of black-and orange-capped bluish-black spots on the hindwing

Compare: Northern Blue (pg. 62) and Melissa Blue (pg. 65)

Comments: The Karner Blue is endangered, its range and population having been reduced due to habitat loss and fire suppression. Michigan and Wisconsin boast the largest populations of this beautiful butterfly.

Appalachian Azure
Celastrina neglectamajor

Family/Subfamily: Gossamer Wings (Lycaenidae)/
Blues (Polyommatinae)

Wingspan: 1.1–1.4" (2.8–3.6 cm)

Habitat: shaded woodlands, forest trails and roadsides

Range: southern Ohio; rare to occasional; localized

Sexes: dissimilar; female has broad forewing borders

Larva: slug-like, variable, green to reddish brown; oblique marks;

Above: male is uniformly light blue with a narrow, dark forewing
border; female is light blue with broad, dark forewing borders
and limited white scaling on hindwing

Below: chalky white with pale, small dark spots and bands;
hindwing has a zigzag band along the margin enclosing
an incomplete row of one to three prominent dark spots

Compare: Summer Azure (pg. 59)

Comments: The Appalachian Azure is our largest resident azure.
It is restricted to the Appalachians. It enters our region in central and southern Ohio. Its colonies are in close association
with Black Baneberry (*Actaea racemosa*), its sole larval host.

ventral

White M Hairstreak
Parrhasius m-album

Family/Subfamily: Gossamer Wings (Lycaenidae)/
Hairstreaks (Theclinae)

Wingspan: 1.25–1.6" (3.2–4.1 cm)

Habitat: open woodlands, forest margins; often near oaks

Range: throughout southern portions of the region; strays
northward; rare to occasional

Sexes: dissimilar; female is duller with reduced blue scaling

Larva: slug-like, variable, dark green to pinkish red

Above: male is a bright blue with broad, black margins; female
is a black with blue scaling limited to wing bases

Below: brownish gray; hindwing has a single red eyespot above
the tail, white spot on leading margin, and a narrow white
line forming a distinct *M* near the red spot

Compare: Oak Hairstreak (pg. 111)

Comments: This is a relatively large hairstreak. It is named for
the narrow white line on the hindwing that forms an *M*.

Frosted Elfin
Callophrys irus

Family/Subfamily: Gossamer Wings (Lycaenidae)/
Hairstreaks (Theclinae)

Wingspan: 0.8–1.0" (2.0–2.5 cm)

Habitat: openings in oak savannas, barrens, forest margins

Range: restricted to scattered populations in Wisconsin,
Michigan, Indiana, and Ohio; rare, localized

Sexes: similar, although the female lacks black forewing stigma

Larva: slug-like, blue green with pale oblique dorsal dashes and
a pale white lateral stripe

Above: unmarked dark brown; male has a dark forewing stigma;
female often has reddish-brown scaling

Below: brown forewing; hindwing is dark brown at base, bordered with white; outer portion lighter with gray along outer
margin; hindwing has a small black spot near the stubby tail

Compare: other Elfin species (pgs. 74, 77, and 89)

Comments: Vulnerable and declining range wide, populations
tend to be very localized and associated with habitats supporting Sundial Lupine (*Lupinus perennis*), its sole larval host.

Compare: Dorcas Copper (pg. 85) is larger, has orange-brown ventral hindwings, and has more-extensive black dorsal spotting; Purplish Copper (pg. 231) is larger and has orange-tan ventral hindwings; female has extensive orange scaling

Comments: Our most diminutive copper is entirely restricted to acidic bogs with an abundance of cranberries. As a result, populations are widespread across the Northeast and portions of the Upper Midwest; they tend to be highly localized but can be abundant when encountered. Adults have a low, weak flight and often alight on low-growing vegetation. They often seek nectar from blossoms of their larval hosts. The Bog Copper has just one generation each year. The eggs overwinter and the larvae complete development the following spring.

Bog Copper

Lycaena epixanthe

Family/Subfamily: Gossamer Wings (Lycaenidae)/
Coppers (Lycaeninae)

Wingspan: 0.75–1.0" (1.9–2.5 cm)

Above: male is brown with purplish iridescence and a prominent black forewing cell spot; hindwing has a narrow orange
zigzag line along the lower margin; female has more
black spotting

Below: light gray with scattered black spots and a narrow
orange zigzag line on outer margin of the hindwing

Sexes: similar, although female has an increased number of
black spots on the wings above

Egg: whitish, turban-shaped, laid singly on host stems or leaves

Larva: slug-like, blue green with a darker green dorsal stripe
and light lateral stripe

Larval Host Plants: Cranberry (*Vaccinium macrocarpon*) and
Small Cranberry (*Vaccinium oxycoccos*)

Habitat: acidic bogs

Broods: single generation; eggs overwinter

Abundance: uncommon to locally common

Range: northern portions of the region in Michigan, Wisconsin,
and Minnesota

Hoary Elfin
Callophrys polios

Family/Subfamily: Gossamer Wings (Lycaenidae)/ Hairstreaks (Theclinae)

Wingspan: 0.8–1.1" (2.0–2.8 cm)

Habitat: forest margins, pine barrens, and adjacent meadows

Range: northern and extreme western portions of the region; occasional; localized

Sexes: similar, although female lacks black forewing stigma

Larva: slug-like, bright green with faint lighter green lines

Above: unmarked dark brown; male has a dark forewing stigma

Below: forewing and hindwing are dark brown at base with extensive violet-gray frosting along outer margin; hindwing has dark postmedian band lacking or with limited white at the ends; no hindwing tails

Compare: Henry's Elfin (pg. 89) and Frosted Elfin (pg. 71)

Comments: This spring-flying species is often found in association with Bearberry (*Arctostaphylos uvaursi*), which is its primary host plant.

Dakota Skipper
Hesperia dacotae

Family/Subfamily: Skippers (Hesperiidae)/
Grass-Skippers (Hesperiinae)

Wingspan: 0.9–1.2" (2.4–3.1 cm)

Habitat: mixed and tallgrass prairie

Range: northwest portions of the region; rare

Sexes: similar

Larva: greenish brown with a white collar and black head

Above: male is tawny orange with dark-brown wing borders and
a black forewing stigma; female is brown with some tawny
orange scaling on the hindwing and pale forewing spots

Below: hindwing is generally an unmarked dull yellow to tawny
in males, occasionally with a faint spot band; hindwing is gray
brown in females with whitish spot band

Compare: other Skippers (pgs. 234, 251 and 262)

Comments: Federally endangered, the Dakota Skipper's popu-
lation has declined due to habitat loss and fragmentation.
Recovery efforts are ongoing. Larvae utilize Little Bluestem
(*Schizachyrium scoparium*) as a host plant.

Compare: Hoary Elfin (pg. 74), Frosted Elfin (pg. 71), and Henry's Elfin (pg. 89) all have noticeable frosting along the outer margin of the ventral hindwing

Comments: The Brown Elfin is a delicate early-spring species with a very short flight period. Populations tend to be scattered, relatively small, and highly localized in close association to stands of their larval hosts. Small size and drab appearance often make individuals easy to overlook. Adults tend to fly close to the ground and often perch on the ends of bare twigs, low vegetation, or on the ground. They feed on nectar on a variety of early-blooming native plants.

Brown Elfin
Callophrys augustinus

Family/Subfamily: Gossamer Wings (Lycaenidae)/ Hairstreaks (Theclinae)

Wingspan: 0.8–1.1" (2.0–2.8 cm)

Above: dark brown; male has a dark forewing stigma

Below: hindwing is dark brown basally, with the outer half a lighter reddish brown to mahogany; smooth margin; lacks hindwing tails

Sexes: similar

Egg: whitish, flattened disc–shaped, laid singly on host flower buds

Larva: slug-like, yellow green with pale oblique dorsal dashes and yellow lateral stripe

Larval Host Plants: various plants in the heath family (Ericaceae), including Mountain Laurel (*Kalmia latifolia*), Leatherleaf (*Chamaedaphne calyculata*), Black Huckleberry (*Gaylussacia baccata*), and blueberry (*Vaccinium* spp.)

Habitat: open woodlands, forest margins and roadsides, and bogs

Broods: single generation; pupae overwinter

Abundance: rare to uncommon; localized

Range: primarily northeastern and southeastern portions of the region

Compare: Crossline Skipper (pg. 99) is larger and usually has a faint band of small, pale spots through the center of the ventral hindwing, plus less-prominent orange scaling along the leading margin of the ventral hindwing in males

Comments: As its name suggests, the Tawny-Edged Skipper has prominent, bright orange scaling along the leading ventral forewing margin that contrasts with the darker hindwing. Although ranging as far west as California, the species is particularly widespread and generally common throughout the eastern US from Florida north to southern Canada. It prefers open, grassy habitats and is often found in somewhat wetter sites. The adults are readily drawn to available flowers.

Tawny-Edged Skipper

Polites themistocles

Family/Subfamily: Skippers (Hesperiidae)/
Grass-Skippers (Hesperiinae)

Wingspan: 0.8–1.2" (2.0–3.0 cm)

Above: dark brown; forewing in male has orange basal scaling, orange scaling along leading margin, and a prominent black stigma with a small orange spot near the tip; forewing in female has somewhat less orange scaling and a few additional orange postmedian spots

Below: somewhat variable; hindwing is light brown to olive brown; forewing has distinct contracting orange scaling along the leading margin and often a few small orange subapical spots

Sexes: similar, although female is darker dorsally, lacks black forewing stigma, and has additional conspicuous orange forewing spots

Egg: greenish white, laid singly on host

Larva: somewhat variable; reddish brown with dark dorsal stripe and black head

Larval Host Plants: various grasses, including Kentucky Bluegrass (*Poa pratensis*), panicgrass (*Panicum* spp.), and crabgrass (*Digitaria* spp.)

Habitat: open, grassy areas, including wet meadows, prairie, stream margins, roadsides, old fields, marshes, yards, and parks

Broods: one to two generations; pupae overwinter

Abundance: occasional to common; locally abundant

Range: throughout

Compare: unique

Comments: The Eufala Skipper is a common, year-round resident of the extreme southern tier of states from Florida to southern California. It regularly wanders well northward to establish temporary breeding colonies but is unable to survive prolonged exposure to freezing temperatures. Individuals have somewhat elongated wings with their ventral surface having a noticeably grayish, washed out appearance. Avid flower visitors, the adults readily nectar at available flowers and frequent gardens. They have a rapid, erratic flight but readily perch on vegetation where they are easily observed.

Eufala Skipper

Lerodea eufala

Family/Subfamily: Skippers (Hesperiidae)/
  Grass-Skippers (Hesperiinae)

Wingspan: 0.8–1.25" (2.0–3.2 cm)

Above: elongated wings; dull dark brown; forewing has a few
  small, glassy light spots

Below: wings are gray brown; forewing has small white subapical
  spots; hindwing unmarked or with faint, pale spot band

Sexes: similar

Egg: cream, laid singly on or near host leaves

Larva: light green with a dark dorsal stripe, light lateral stripes
  and a cream head marked by brown

Larval Host Plants: various grasses, including Johnsongrass
  (*Sorghum halepense*) and Bermudagrass (*Cynodon dactylon*)

Habitat: forest margins, fields, roadsides, yards, and gardens

Broods: two or more generations in the south; does not overwinter in our region

Abundance: rare; stray or temporary colonizer

Range: extreme southern portions of the region;
  strays northward

Compare: Western Pine Elfin (pg. 107) also has a very heavily patterned ventral hindwing, but banding is generally darker and more jagged

Comments: With its boldly patterned hindwings, this spring species is one of our most distinctive elfins. While widespread across many portions of the region, it is seldom encountered in large numbers and tends to be found in close association with younger pine trees. Adults spend much of their time perched on sunlit branches, often high above the ground, but frequently venture to nearby flowers. Males often puddle at damp earth.

Eastern Pine Elfin

Callophrys niphon

Family/Subfamily: Gossamer Wings (Lycaenidae)/ Hairstreaks (Theclinae)

Wingspan: 0.8–1.25" (2.0–3.2 cm)

Above: male unmarked, dark brown with pale gray forewing stigma; female brown with increased orange scaling; hindwing lacks tail

Below: brown, strongly banded with blackish brown, reddish brown, gray, and white; hindwing has a distinct gray marginal band

Sexes: similar, although female is tawnier and lacks forewing stigma

Egg: pale green, flattened disc–shaped, laid singly at base of host needles

Larva: slug-like, bright green with longitudinal white stripes

Larval Host Plants: various pines (*Pinus* spp.), including Eastern White Pine (*Pinus strobus*) and Jack Pine (*Pinus banksiana*)

Habitat: open woodlands, pine barrens, forest margins, wooded roadsides and easements, and brushy fields

Broods: single generation; pupae overwinter

Abundance: occasional; localized

Range: throughout eastern portions of the range; absent from Iowa, North Dakota, South Dakota, and Nebraska

Compare: Purplish Copper (pg. 231) is larger and has distinct orange submarginal line on dorsal hindwing; females have more extensive orange dorsal scaling; Bog Copper (pg. 73) is smaller and restricted to acid bogs with cranberries

Comments: This primarily boreal species essentially replaces the Purplish Copper northward into Canada. A butterfly of wet, often shrubby habitats, it is intensely localized but often common when encountered. Adults seldom venture far from patches of their larval host plants. They have a weak flight and often alight on low vegetation with their wings partially open. Both sexes are fond of flowers and may be closely observed while feeding.

Dorcas Copper

Tharsalea dorcas

Family/Subfamily: Gossamer Wings (Lycaenidae)/ Coppers (Lycaeninae)

Wingspan: 0.85–1.20" (2.2–3.0 cm)

Above: male is brown with purplish iridescence and scattered small black spots; female is brown (occasionally with a hint of orange) with several scattered black spots

Below: forewing is yellow orange with orange-brown apex and scattered black spots; hindwing is somewhat variable; light orange brown with scattered small black spots and a narrow, zigzagging, orange submarginal band

Sexes: dissimilar; female is dull brown with a small amount of orange scaling on the wings above

Egg: greenish white, turban-shaped, laid singly on host leaves

Larva: slug-like, light green with darker green dorsal stripe and pale oblique dashes

Larval Host Plants: Shrubby Cinquefoil (*Dasiphora fruticosa*)

Habitat: open, shrubby sites, including meadows, bogs, seeps, stream margins, fens, and wet roadsides

Broods: single generation; eggs overwinter

Abundance: occasional to common; localized

Range: northern portions of the region in Michigan, Wisconsin, and Minnesota

Compare: unique

Comments: This drab brown butterfly is distinctly plain and can reliably identified by its olive to yellow-brown ventral coloration and light veins. That said, its small size and uninspiring appearance make the Swarthy Skipper easy to overlook in the field. Widely distributed throughout the southeastern US and Mid-Atlantic, it enters the southern portion of our region but is often infrequently encountered. Colonies are often somewhat localized near host patches. Adults have a very rapid, erratic flight and frequently visit flowers. The long, narrow larvae construct individual tube-like shelters on the host by rolling grass blades over lengthwise.

Swarthy Skipper
Nastra lherminier

Family/Subfamily: Skippers (Hesperiidae)/
Grass-Skippers (Hesperiinae)

Wingspan: 0.9–1.1" (2.3–2.8 cm)

Above: dull dark brown; forewing occasionally has a faint
pale spot

Below: dull olive brown to yellow brown with light veins

Sexes: similar

Egg: white, laid singly on host leaves

Larva: elongated; pale green with a darker green dorsal stripe;
head is reddish-brown with cream stripes

Larval Host Plants: various grasses, including Little Bluestem
(*Schizachyrium scoparium*)

Habitat: woodland margins and openings, old fields, meadows,
roadsides, utility easements, and other disturbed sites

Broods: two generations; larvae overwinter

Abundance: uncommon to occasional

Range: southern portions of the range; rare to absent in northern and western portions

Compare: Frosted Elfin (pg. 71) has a relatively straight, dark postmedian band on the ventral forewing and typically has a dark ventral hindwing spot near the stubby tail; Hoary Elfin (pg. 74) lacks a stubby hindwing tail and has more-extensive frosting along the outer margins of wings below.

Comments: This is our most widespread and frequently encountered elfin, especially in southern portions of the region. An early-spring species, Henry's Elfin can be found in a variety of semiopen areas, often in close association with stands of its larval hosts. As a result, the butterfly tends to be spotty and rather local but can be fairly numerous when encountered. Population numbers often vary considerably from year to year. Adults have a quick, erratic flight and regularly perch on the tips of small tree branches or on low, shrubby vegetation. They frequently nectar at available blooms.

Henry's Elfin
Callophrys henrici

Family/Subfamily: Gossamer Wings (Lycaenidae)/
Hairstreaks (Theclinae)

Wingspan: 0.9–1.2" (2.3–3.0 cm)

Above: warm to dark brown with amber-orange scaling along
outer margin of wings; hindwing has short, stubby tail;
males lack black forewing stigma

Below: brown; hindwing is distinctly two-toned with dark-
brown basal half and light-brown outer half; gray frosting
along outer margin

Sexes: similar

Egg: whitish, flattened disc-shaped, laid singly on host twigs or
flower buds

Larva: slug-like, variable; green to reddish with oblique pale
dorsal markings

Larval Host Plants: Mapleleaf Viburnum (*Viburnum acerifolium*),
Redbud (*Cercis canadensis*), Carolina Buckthorn (*Rhamnus
caroliniana*), and holly (*Ilex* spp.) may be used across its range.

Habitat: deciduous woodlands, barrens, forest margins and
clearings, easements, and shrubby areas.

Broods: single generation; pupae overwinter

Abundance: occasional; localized

Range: throughout

Compare: Common Roadside-Skipper (pg. 109) lacks the white ventral hindwing band

Comments: This small skipper is well named—its ventral wing surfaces indeed look as if they were sprinkled with salt and pepper. Although widespread throughout the East, it tends to be a universally uncommon butterfly. It is most often encountered individually or in small numbers, darting in and out of woodland openings or along forested roadways. The adults speed along near the ground with a rapid and somewhat erratic flight. Males often imbibe moisture and other nutrients from damp earth.

Pepper and Salt Skipper

Amblyscirtes hegon

Family/Subfamily: Skippers (Hesperiidae)/
Grass-Skippers (Hesperiinae)

Wingspan: 0.9–1.2" (2.3–3.0 cm)

Above: dark brown with checkered fringes; forewing has a band of small white spots

Below: variable; hindwing is greenish gray with a white postmedian spot band and checkered fringes

Sexes: similar

Egg: light green, laid singly on host leaves

Larva: whitish green with a dark-green dorsal stripe, a light lateral stripe, and a reddish-brown head marked with light brown

Larval Host Plants: various grasses, including Indiangrass (*Sorghastrum nutans*), Kentucky Bluegrass (*Poa pratensis*), and Indian Woodoats (*Chasmanthium latifolium*)

Habitat: sunlit forest clearings, forest margins and trails, glades, stream corridors, and adjacent open areas

Broods: one generation; larvae overwinter

Abundance: uncommon to occasional; local

Range: central and eastern portions of the region

Northern Metalmark
Calephelis borealis

Family/Subfamily: Metalmarks (Riodinidae)/
True Metalmarks (Riodininae)

Wingspan: 0.9–1.2" (2.3–3.0 cm)

Habitat: rocky woodlands and slopes, outcrops, forest margins, and adjacent stream margins, clearings, and disturbed sites

Range: Ohio and Missouri within our region; rare; localized

Sexes: similar, although female has broader, rounder wings

Larva: green with tiny black spots; covered in long whitish hairs; single generation; partially grown larvae overwinter

Above: brown to reddish brown with numerous dark markings and two narrow, metallic silvery-gray bands along the outer edge of the wings; inner half of wings darker brown

Below: marked similarly to dorsal surface but a brighter orange

Compare: Swamp Metalmark (pg. 225)

Comments: Exists close to patches of Roundleaf Ragwort (*Packera obovata*), its larval host. Vulnerable to habitat loss and should be conserved. Adults have a low, weak flight and regularly alight on vegetation with their wings spread.

Poweshiek Skipperling
Oarisma Poweshiek

Family/Subfamily: Skippers (Hesperiidae)/
Grass-Skippers (Hesperiinae)

Wingspan: 0.9–1.2" (2.3–3.0 cm)

Habitat: prairie, sedge meadows, and fens

Range: Dakotas to Michigan; rare

Sexes: similar

Larva: green with cream-yellow longitudinal stripes and a green head; one generation; larvae overwinter

Above: rich dark brown with tawny scaling along the leading margin of the forewing; short antennae

Below: hindwing is gray brown with white veins

Compare: unique

Comments: The Poweshiek Skipperling is historically found across the Upper Midwest from the Dakotas and Iowa east to Michigan and northern Indiana. Rare, declining, and federally listed as endangered. Recovery efforts are ongoing. Hosts include Little Bluestem (*Schizachyrium scoparium*) and Prairie Dropseed (*Sporobolus heterolepis*).

Compare: unique

Comments: The Common Sootywing indeed looks as if it fell into a pail of ashes. Widespread throughout much of the US, it is a butterfly of open, disturbed sites where its weedy, nonnative larval hosts regularly invade. Periodic strays often colonize locations farther north, including into southern Canada. Adults have a low, erratic flight and scurry around quickly, stopping to feed or perch with their glossy black wings outstretched. The larvae construct individual shelters on the host by folding over leaves with silk.

Common Sootywing

Pholisora catullus

Family/Subfamily: Skippers (Hesperiidae)/
Spread-Wing Skippers (Pyrginae)

Wingspan: 0.9–1.25" (2.3–3.2 cm)

Above: slightly shiny, dark brown to black, with variable number
of small white spots on the forewing and top of the head

Below: as above but somewhat paler

Sexes: similar, although female has somewhat larger white
forewing spots

Egg: reddish pink, laid singly on the underside of host leaves

Larva: pale gray-green with narrow dorsal stripe, pale-green
lateral stripes, a black collar, and a bulbous black head;
body is covered in tiny yellow-white spots

Larval Host Plants: Lambsquarter (*Chenopodium album*),
Mexican Tea (*Dysphania ambrosioides*), and Slim Amaranth
(*Amaranthus hybridus*)

Habitat: open, disturbed sites, including roadsides, weedy fields,
fallow agricultural lands, and utility easements

Broods: one or more generations; larvae overwinter

Abundance: occasional; local

Range: southern two-thirds of the region; uncommon or rare
in far northern portions

Lace-Winged Roadside-Skipper
Amblyscirtes aesculapius

Family/Subfamily: Skippers (Hesperiidae)/
Grass-Skippers (Hesperiinae)

Wingspan: 1.0–1.2" (2.5–3.0 cm)

Habitat: moist hardwood forests, bottomland forests, and
shaded stream corridors

Range: extreme southern portions of the region; rare to
uncommon; local

Sexes: similar

Larva: light green to almost gray with a dark dorsal stripe;
pinkish-tan head marked with black and brown

Above: dull dark brown; forewing has a central band of tiny
white spots; wing fringes are checkered

Below: hindwing is dark brown with white veins intersected by
irregular white spot bands forming a lacy pattern

Compare: unique

Comments: Populations are found near stands of cane (*Arundin-
aria* spp.), their known larval host. The adults perch on
vegetation and seek nectar at a variety of available flowers.

ventral

Clouded Skipper
Lerema accius

Family/Subfamily: Skippers (Hesperiidae)/
Grass-Skippers (Hesperiinae)

Wingspan: 1.0–1.5" (2.5–3.8 cm)

Habitat: wooded areas, wetlands, grasslands, and yards

Range: primarily extreme southern portions of the region; strays temporarily colonize northward

Sexes: similar, although female has large forewing spots

Larva: green with dark dorsal stripe and white head; black-and-white stripes and white spots

Above: dark brown; forewing has several small, semitransparent white spots; hindwing is unmarked

Below: dark brown; forewing has a row of small, semitransparent white spots below the apex; both wings have lavender-gray scaling in the center and along the outer margin

Compare: Zabulon Skipper (pg. 123)

Comments: Our only member of this primarily tropical genus. It is widespread and common throughout the Southeast. The larvae utilize various grass species as hosts.

Compare: Tawny-Edged Skipper (pg. 79) is smaller; typically lacks the faint band of small, pale spots through the center of the ventral hindwing; and has prominent orange scaling along the leading margin of the forewing that contrasts with the darker hindwing

Comments: Although widespread throughout much of the East, this species is seldom very common. Colonies tend to be rather small and often quite local. It generally tends to be found in drier habitats than the similar-looking and more abundant Tawny-edged Skipper with which it (particularly males) can be confused. Adults have a low, rapid flight and often alight on grasses and other low growing vegetation. Larvae construct individual leaf shelters on the host grasses.

Crossline Skipper

Polites origenes

Family/Subfamily: Skippers (Hesperiidae)/
Grass-Skippers (Hesperiinae)

Wingspan: 1.0–1.25" (2.5–3.2 cm)

Above: dark brown; forewing in male has orange basal scaling, orange scaling along leading margin, and a prominent black stigma with a few small, orange postmedian spots; forewing in female is primarily brown with a few pale spots

Below: hindwing is orange brown to olive brown with a post-median band of light, often-faint spots; forewing primarily in males often has dull-orange scaling along leading margin not strongly contrasting with hindwing

Sexes: dissimilar; females darker above and the forewing lacks orange scaling along the leading margin and a black stigma

Egg: greenish white, laid singly on host

Larva: dark brown with faint white mottling; black head has a cream collar

Larval Host Plants: various grasses, including Purpletop Tridens (*Tridens flavus*), Little Bluestem (*Schizachyrium scoparium*), and mannagrass (*Glyceria* spp.)

Habitat: dry, grassy areas, including forest margins and clearings, barrens, old fields, pastures, prairies, and suburban parks and yards

Broods: one to two generations; larvae overwinter

Abundance: uncommon to occasional; local

Range: eastern and southern portions of the region; uncommon or absent north and west

Compare: unique

Comments: Aptly named, this small, dark skipper has subtle but distinctly scalloped wing margins, making it easy to recognize. Although widespread throughout much of the Southeast, populations seem to be fairly localized and never overly abundant. Adults perch on low, often sun-dappled vegetation with their wings spread. They seek nectar from a variety of small flowers and may occasionally be spotted in gardens. The larvae construct individual shelters on the host by tying several leaves together with silk.

Hayhurst's Scallopwing
Staphylus hayhurstii

Family/Subfamily: Skippers (Hesperiidae)/
Spread-Wing Skippers (Pyrginae)

Wingspan: 1.0–1.25" (2.5–3.2 cm)

Above: wings are a dark brownish black with scattered white
flecks and a few, mainly subapical, small white forewing
spots; wing margins are noticeably scalloped

Below: as above but somewhat paler

Sexes: similar, although male is somewhat darker above

Egg: reddish pink, laid singly on the underside of host leaves

Larva: pale gray green with tiny white spots and a bulbous black
head; body is covered in tiny yellow-white spots

Larval Host Plants: Lambsquarters (*Chenopodium album*)

Habitat: woodland openings, trails and margins, stream margins,
roadsides, weedy fields, utility easements, and yards

Broods: two generations; larvae overwinter

Abundance: occasional; local

Range: southern portions of the region

Compare: Edwards' Hairstreak (pg. 117) has a row of white-rimmed black spots—not dashes—on wings below; Banded Hairstreak (pg. 115) is extremely similar, but the blue ventral hindwing patch does not extend as far inward

Comments: The Hickory Hairstreak is a reclusive and uncommon butterfly of rich mixed deciduous forests and second-growth woodlands. As its name implies, the larvae primarily utilize a number of hickory species as hosts. Populations tend to be small and highly localized in occurrence. In addition to its rarity, this butterfly may be easily overlooked due to its close resemblance to the more widespread and common Banded Hairstreak, with which it often flies. Like many other hair-streaks, adults are particularly fond of milkweed blossoms.

Hickory Hairstreak

Satyrium caryaevorus

Family/Subfamily: Gossamer Wings (Lycaenidae)/
Hairstreaks (Theclinae)

Wingspan: 1.0–1.25" (2.5–3.2 cm)

Above: unmarked; dark brown; male has a small gray
forewing stigma

Below: brown with row of fairly wide and somewhat offset dark
dashes edged in white across both wings; hindwing has a
large blue patch and orange-capped black spot near the tail

Sexes: similar, although male has a forewing stigma

Egg: pinkish brown, flattened disc–shaped, laid singly on
host twigs

Larva: slug-like, yellow green, often with darker green dorsal
stripe, a yellow lateral stripe, and dark dashes edged in white

Larval Host Plants: various hickories (*Carya* spp.), including
Shagbark Hickory (*Carya ovata*), Pignut Hickory (*Carya
glabra*), and Bitternut Hickory (*Carya cordiformis*); also
American Chestnut (*Castanea dentata*)

Habitat: mixed deciduous forests, forest clearings, adjacent
fields, roadsides, and semiopen brushy areas

Broods: single generation; eggs overwinter

Abundance: rare to occasional to common

Range: throughout most of the region; absent from northern
and westernmost areas

Compare: unique

Comments: This small and conspicuous species is widespread and generally one of the more common skippers throughout our region, being quite abundant at times in the right situations. Primarily a butterfly of moist habitats, it tolerates a wide range of human-disturbed, grassy landscapes, including those in more-urbanized settings. The small adults maneuver close to the ground with a darting, rapid flight but regularly alight on vegetation or visit available flowers. The distinctive ventral hindwing patch is somewhat variable in appearance and may be continuous or broken into separate spots.

Peck's Skipper
Polites peckius

Family/Subfamily: Skippers (Hesperiidae)/
Grass-Skippers (Hesperiinae)

Wingspan: 1.0–1.25" (2.5–3.2 cm)

Above: dark olive brown; hindwing has elongated central spots; male forewing has orange scaling along inner half of leading margin, a few tiny spots toward the apex, and a prominent black stigma; female has additional and more-prominent orange forewing spots

Below: somewhat variable; hindwing is dark brown with a distinctive, irregular, golden median patch, with the central elongated spot extending out farther than the rest

Sexes: similar, although female lacks black forewing stigma and has additional conspicuous orange forewing spots

Egg: cream, laid singly on host

Larva: dark maroon brown with a black head and anal patch

Larval Host Plants: various grasses, including Rice Cutgrass (*Leersia oryzoides*) and Kentucky Bluegrass (*Poa pratensis*)

Habitat: open, grassy areas, including wet meadows, roadsides, old fields, marshes, yards, and parks

Broods: two or more generations each year; larvae and/or pupae overwinter

Abundance: occasional to common

Range: throughout

Compare: Eastern Pine Elfin (pg. 83) also has a very heavily patterned ventral hindwing, but its banding is generally lighter and less jagged

Comments: As its name implies, the Western Pine Elfin is widely distributed across western portions of the US. It just creeps into extreme western portions of our region with limited records farther east in northern Minnesota, Wisconsin, and the Upper Peninsula of Michigan. Additional monitoring should be done to increase our understanding of this butterfly's presence within the Upper Midwest. As for now, sightings of the Western Pine Elfin in the region represent a good find for butterfliers.

Western Pine Elfin

Callophrys eryphon

Family/Subfamily: Gossamer Wings (Lycaenidae)/ Hairstreaks (Theclinae)

Wingspan: 1.0–1.25" (2.5–3.2 cm)

Above: unmarked dark brown with orange scaling; hindwing lacks tail; male lacks forewing stigma

Below: brown, strongly banded with blackish brown, reddish brown, gray, and white; submarginal band strongly jagged

Sexes: similar

Egg: pale green, flattened disc–shaped, laid singly at base of host needles

Larva: slug-like, bright green with cream-white stripes running along the side

Larval Host Plants: various pines (*Pinus* spp.), likely Lodgepole Pine (*Pinus contorta*) and Ponderosa Pine (*Pinus ponderosa*); unknown in eastern portion

Habitat: open pine woodlands, pine barrens, and forest margins

Broods: single generation; pupae overwinter

Abundance: rare; localized

Range: extreme western portion of the region; records from upper Minnesota, Wisconsin, and Michigan

Compare: Pepper and Salt Skipper (pg. 91) has a ventral hind-wing white band; Linda's Roadside-Skipper (pg. 139) is geographically restricted and has some white spotting on the ventral hindwing

Comments: This drab species is the most widespread roadside-skipper in the US and certainly in our region. Nonetheless, populations are generally uncommon and highly localized, with adults typically being encountered alone or in small numbers. The larvae construct individual leaf shelters on the host. Males frequently perch on low vegetation or are spotted puddling at moist ground.

Common Roadside-Skipper

Amblyscirtes vialis

Family/Subfamily: Skippers (Hesperiidae)/
Grass-Skippers (Hesperiinae)

Wingspan: 1.0–1.3" (2.5–3.3 cm)

Above: dark brown with checkered fringes; forewing has a few small white spots near the apex

Below: hindwing is dark brown with purplish frosting on the outer half; forewing has a few small subapical spots or triangular spot band

Sexes: similar

Egg: light green, laid singly on host leaves

Larva: whitish green with a light-gray head marked with reddish-brown lines

Larval Host Plants: various grasses, including bluegrasses (*Poa* spp.), bentgrasses (*Agrostis* spp.), and Indian Woodoats (*Chasmanthium latifolium*)

Habitat: sunlit forest clearings, forest margins and trails, glades, barrens, stream corridors, and adjacent open areas

Broods: one generation; larvae overwinter

Abundance: uncommon to occasional; local

Range: throughout

Compare: White M Hairstreak (pg. 70) is larger, is iridescent blue above, and has a single prominent red spot on the ventral hindwing

Comments: Although previously seen as separate species (the Oak or Northern Oak Hairstreak), populations outside of peninsular Florida and the extreme southern Atlantic Coast are now recognized as geographic races of the same species. Closely associated with oak-dominated woodlands or barrens, populations tend to be generally small and fairly localized when encountered. The adults often reside high in the tree canopy but venture down periodically to feed at available flowering plants.

Oak Hairstreak

Satyrium favonius

Family/Subfamily: Gossamer Wings (Lycaenidae)/
Hairstreaks (Theclinae)

Wingspan: 1.0–1.3" (2.5–3.3 cm)

Above: dark brown with a small orange spot near the tail; male
has dark forewing stigma

Below: gray brown with a white postmedian line strongly zigzagging near hindwing tail; hindwing has a large blue patch
often capped lightly in orange and an orange-capped black
spot near the tail

Sexes: similar

Egg: pinkish brown, flattened disc–shaped, laid singly on host
twigs and buds

Larva: slug-like, pale green

Larval Host Plants: various oaks (*Quercus* spp.), including
Northern Red Oak (*Quercus rubra*), Post Oak (*Quercus
stellata*), and White Oak (*Quercus* alba)

Habitat: open woodlands, forest margins, and adjacent open
or semiopen sites near oaks

Broods: one generation; eggs overwinter

Abundance: rare to occasional

Range: throughout southeastern portions of the region

Bell's Roadside-Skipper
Amblyscirtes belli

Family/Subfamily: Skippers (Hesperiidae)/
Grass-Skippers (Hesperiinae)

Wingspan: 1.0–1.3" (2.5–3.3 cm)

Habitat: moist hardwood forests, margins, and openings

Range: extreme southern portions; rare to uncommon; local

Sexes: similar

Larva: light green to grayish with a cream head marked by a
brown stripe

Above: dull dark brown; forewing has a central band of tiny
white spots; wing fringes are checkered

Below: hindwing is dark brown with one to two white spot
bands; wing fringes are checkered; forewing has small white
subapical spots; has gray frosting along outer wing margins

Compare: Linda's Roadside-Skipper (pg. 139), Pepper and Salt
Skipper (pg. 91), and Common Roadside-Skipper (pg. 109)

Comments: Populations tend to be localized and easy to overlook. The larvae feed on Indian Woodoats (*Chasmanthium
latifolium*) and construct individual leaf shelters.

Funereal Duskywing
Erynnis funeralis

Family/Subfamily: Skippers (Hesperiidae)/
Spread-Wing Skippers (Pyrginae)

Wingspan: 1.0–1.5" (2.5–3.8 cm)

Habitat: woodland edges, fields, roadsides, and gardens

Range: strays into our region and may temporarily colonize southern portions; rare

Sexes: similar

Larva: light green with a yellow lateral stripe; head is brown with orange spots around the margin; covered in tiny white spots

Above: dark chocolate brown; forewing is very dark with a prominent brown patch at the end of the cell and a few small, subapical glassy spots; hindwing has contrasting white fringe

Below: dark brown; hindwing has two rows of small pale spots

Compare: unique—this is the only duskywing with distinct white hindwing fringes

Comments: Primarily a butterfly of the southwestern US, it regularly wanders east and north, straying or colonizing locations. Larvae feed on plants in the pea family (Fabaceae).

Compare: Edwards' Hairstreak (pg. 117) has a row of white-rimmed black spots, not dashes, below; Hickory Hairstreak (pg. 103), which is extremely similar and may not reliably be separated in the field, typically has ventral blue hindwing patch extending farther inward and more-offset, dark post-median band on ventral forewing

Comments: This diminutive species is one of our most common hairstreaks. A butterfly of mixed deciduous forests, the adults are fond of flowers and may be found feeding at available blooms in nearby fields and clearings. It can also be encountered in more-urbanized locations, including parks and gardens, if the larval host trees are nearby. Males often perch on shrubs or low, overhanging limbs and aggressively dart out to investigate other passing individuals.

Banded Hairstreak

Satyrium calanus

Family/Subfamily: Gossamer Wings (Lycaenidae)/
Hairstreaks (Theclinae)

Wingspan: 1.0–1.35" (2.5–3.4 cm)

Above: unmarked dark brown

Below: gray brown with rows of white-outlined dark dashes
across both wings; hindwing has a blue patch and red-
capped black spot near tail

Sexes: similar

Egg: pinkish brown, flattened disc–shaped, laid singly on host
twigs near the buds

Larva: slug-like, variable, green to gray brown to tan with a light
lateral stripe and occasionally some dark dorsal markings

Larval Host Plants: various oaks (*Quercus* spp.), including White
Oak (*Quercus alba*), Northern Red Oak (*Quercus rubra*), and
Chestnut Oak (*Quercus montana*); also Shagbark Hickory
(*Carya ovata*), Pignut Hickory (*Carya glabra*), Butternut
(*Juglans cinerea*), and Black Walnut (*Juglans nigra*)

Habitat: mixed deciduous forests, oak woodlands, forest
clearings and margins, parks, utility easements, roadsides,
and gardens

Broods: single generation; eggs overwinter

Abundance: occasional to common

Range: throughout most of the region; absent or rare in
westernmost areas

Compare: Striped Hairstreak (pg. 119) and Banded Hairstreak (pg. 115) have bands of white-edged dashes—not distinctly separated spots—on the wings below; Acadian Hairstreak (pg. 217) is grayer below and restricted to moist habitats with willows

Comments: Edwards' Hairstreak is associated with dry areas dominated by short, scrubby oaks. Its short flight period and close resemblance to other, more common hairstreaks can make the butterfly easy to overlook. The slug-like larvae are regularly tended (and guarded from predators) by ants (typically *Formica* spp.). Older larvae spend the day in ant structures at the base of host trees and venture out at night to feed. The reliance on ants may contribute to the butterfly's spotty and localized distribution. Like other hairstreaks, the adults are readily attracted to milkweed blossoms.

Edwards' Hairstreak
Satyrium edwardsii

Family/Subfamily: Gossamer Wings (Lycaenidae)/ Hairstreaks (Theclinae)

Wingspan: 1.0–1.35" (2.5–3.4 cm)

Above: unmarked dark brown with a small orange spot near the tail; male has a small dark forewing stigma

Below: light gray-brown with row of small, white-rimmed black spots; hindwing has a large blue patch and a series of orange spots near the tail

Sexes: similar, although male has forewing stigma; female has more rounded wings

Egg: creamy tinged with pink, flattened disc-shaped, laid singly on host twigs near the buds

Larva: slug-like, dark brown with a dark dorsal band and a series of pale oblique dashes along the sides

Larval Host Plants: various oaks (*Quercus* spp.), including Black Oak (*Quercus velutina*), Scarlet Oak (*Quercus coccinea*), Blackjack Oak (*Quercus marilandica*), White Oak (*Quercus alba*), and Bur Oak (*Quercus macrocarpa*)

Habitat: prairie hills, ridges, oak savanna and barrens, oak woodland openings, margins, and trails, hedgerows, and utility easements

Broods: single generation; eggs overwinter

Abundance: uncommon to common; localized

Range: throughout most of the region; absent or rare in westernmost areas

Compare: Banded Hairstreak (pg. 115) and Hickory Hairstreak (pg. 103) have less-extensive, narrower ventral banding and lack orange cap over blue hindwing patch, and they also lack the white-rimmed black spots; Edwards' Hairstreak (pg. 117) has a row of white-rimmed black spots—not dashes—below

Comments: The Striped Hairstreak's name comes from the numerous, white-edged dark bands that give the wings below an overall striped appearance. Although widespread throughout the Midwest, it is generally uncommon and seldom seen in large numbers. In fact, it is considered vulnerable or imperiled in several eastern states. The handsome adults are often encountered alongside other similar-looking hairstreaks on available flowers.

Striped Hairstreak
Satyrium liparops

Family/Subfamily: Gossamer Wings (Lycaenidae)/
Hairstreaks (Theclinae)

Wingspan: 1.0–1.35" (2.5–3.4 cm)

Above: unmarked dark brown

Below: brown to brown gray with numerous wide, dark bands
outlined in white; hindwing has an orange-capped black spot
and blue patch near the tail

Sexes: similar

Egg: pinkish brown, flattened disc–shaped, laid singly on
host twigs

Larva: slug-like, bright green with a yellow-green lateral stripe

Larval Host Plants: various trees and shrubs in the heath
(Ericaceae) and rose (Rosaceae) families, including Black
Cherry (*Prunus serotina*), Pin Cherry (*Prunus pensylvanica*),
Farkleberry (*Vaccinium arboretum*), Highbush Blueberry
(*Vaccinium corymbosum*), and serviceberry (*Amelanchier* spp.)

Habitat: mixed deciduous forests, thickets, woodland clearings
and margins, and adjacent open areas

Broods: single generation; eggs overwinter

Abundance: rare to occasional; localized

Range: throughout the region

Compare: unique

Comments: A reclusive butterfly, the Mulberry Wing occurs in a patchwork range from southern Maine and Quebec west across the Upper Great Lakes to central Minnesota and Iowa. It is a small and distinctive skipper of sedge-dominated freshwater wetlands. Restricted by habitat, it typically occurs in small and highly localized populations that can often be easily overlooked. It remains poorly known, with limited detail of its overall biology. Adults flutter low with a slow, weak flight amongst the wetland vegetation. They alight frequently and are most often observed at nearby flowers or when flushed into the air.

Mulberry Wing
Poanes massasoit

Family/Subfamily: Skippers (Hesperiidae)/
Grass-Skippers (Hesperiinae)

Wingspan: 1.0–1.4" (2.5–3.6 cm)

Above: dark blackish brown; male is virtually unmarked; female
has a few yellow forewing spots and a yellow central spot
band on the hindwing

Below: forewing has a few small, yellow subapical spots;
hindwing is a dark reddish brown with a golden-yellow
postmedian spot band intersected by a long central ray

Sexes: similar, although female has increased yellow spots
on the wings above

Egg: white, laid singly on host

Larva: poorly known

Larval Host Plants: various sedges, including Upright Sedge
(*Carex stricta*)

Habitat: freshwater wetlands, including swamps, fens, marshes,
wet grassy meadows, roadside ditches, and stream margins

Broods: one generation; overwintering stage is unknown

Abundance: uncommon to occasional; local

Range: primarily northeast portion of the region

female

Compare: Hobomok Skipper (pg. 165) male has clear ventral hindwing spot band; ventral hindwing in female lacks the white bar along the upper angle

Comments: The Zabulon Skipper is a distinctly dimorphic species, with orange males and dark-brown females. Widespread throughout much of the eastern US, it overlaps or replaces the similar-looking Hobomok Skipper in southern portions of the region. A denizen of more-wooded habitats, adults are frequently encountered along sun-dappled forest margins and trails as well as in nearby open areas. The pugnacious males perch on branches to await passing females and aggressively engage rivals. Females generally prefer to remain within the confines of shadier locales. Larvae construct individual leaf shelters on the host.

Zabulon Skipper

Poanes zabulon

Family/Subfamily: Skippers (Hesperiidae)/
Grass-Skippers (Hesperiinae)

Wingspan: 1.0–1.4" (2.5–3.6 cm)

Above: male is yellow orange with broad dark-brown wing
borders; female is dark brown with pale yellow-orange
forewing spots

Below: male hindwing is yellow with a brown margin, a brown
base enclosing a yellow spot, and scattered, small brown
central spots; female is dark brown; forewing has small white
subapical spots and purplish-gray frosting; hindwing has
broad purplish-gray frosting along outer margin in the lower
center of the wing, along with a narrow white bar along the
outer angle

Sexes: dissimilar; female is dark brown above and below; small
yellow-orange spots are limited to the dorsal forewing

Egg: white, laid singly on host

Larva: brown green with a tan head and white collar

Larval Host Plants: various grasses, including Purpletop Tridens
(*Tridens flavus*), Whitegrass (*Leersia virginica*), orchardgrass
(*Dactylis* spp.), and bentgrass (*Agrostis* spp.)

Habitat: open woodlands, forest margins and adjacent trails,
stream corridors, nearby roadsides, open areas, and
occasionally gardens

Broods: two generations; larvae likely overwinter

Abundance: uncommon to common

Range: primarily southern half of the region; rare in far west

Compare: Acadian Hairstreak (pg. 217) is light gray below and has prominent hindwing tail

Comments: Upon close inspection, this distinctive tailless hairstreak is unlikely to be confused with any other small butterfly in the region. Adults frequent a variety of semiopen, shrubby habitats in close association with their somewhat aggressive, thicket-forming hosts. Both sexes avidly visit flowers and are exceedingly fond of milkweed blossoms, which they are often observed feeding on alongside other butterflies. The larvae are nocturnal, coming out at night to crawl up host trees and feed.

Coral Hairstreak

Satyrium titus

Family/Subfamily: Gossamer Wings (Lycaenidae)/
Hairstreaks (Theclinae)

Wingspan: 1.0–1.5" (2.5–3.8 cm)

Above: unmarked brown; male has a small gray forewing stigma

Below: light grayish brown with row of small, white-rimmed
black dots across both wings; hindwing has a row of coral
spots along the outer margin; hindwing lacks a tail

Sexes: similar, although male has a forewing stigma and more
triangular wings

Egg: cream, flattened disc–shaped, laid singly on host twigs, low
in the trunks of small host trees, or occasionally in leaf litter
below the host

Larva: slug-like, bright green with pinkish patches on each end;
larvae are associated with ants

Larval Host Plants: Wild Cherry (*Prunus serotina*), Chokecherry
(*Prunus virginiana*), and American Plum (*Prunus americana*);
additional hosts may be used

Habitat: overgrown fields near forest margins, brushy woodland clearings, shrubby roadsides, easements and trails,
and fencerows

Broods: single generation; eggs overwinter

Abundance: occasional to common

Range: throughout

ventral

Compare: Little Glassywing (pg. 129) has distinct glassy white dorsal forewing spots and typically a noticeable but faint ventral hindwing spot band; Northern Broken-Dash (pg. 131) has a prominent ventral hindwing spot band

Comments: The Dun Skipper is a small, dull, and virtually unmarked chocolate-brown butterfly. Although preferring moist, grassy, or sedge-dominated areas in or near deciduous woodlands, the adults, particularly males, readily venture into adjacent open upland habitats and can even be found in gardens. Females often prefer shadier confines. Widespread and generally common, it can at times be locally quite abundant. Adults have a quick, low flight and are avid flower visitors.

Dun Skipper

Euphyes vestris

Family/Subfamily: Skippers (Hesperiidae)/
Grass-Skippers (Hesperiinae)

Wingspan: 1.0–1.5" (2.5–3.8 cm)

Above: male is dark chocolate brown; forewing has a black stigma and some faint tawny basal scaling; forewing in female has a few (generally two) pale central spots

Below: hindwing typically is unmarked, dark chocolate brown; occasionally has a faint curved central spot band

Sexes: similar, but female has a few pale dorsal forewing spots

Egg: light green, laid singly on host

Larva: green with fine white mottling; brown head is marked with cream lines around the margin, a black oval on the top, and a black collar

Larval Host Plants: various sedges (*Carex* spp.)

Habitat: moist areas in or near deciduous woodlands, forest margins, swamps, and adjacent open areas

Broods: one to two generations; larvae overwinter

Abundance: occasional to common; local

Range: throughout

Compare: Northern Broken-Dash (pg. 131) lacks the prominent dorsal forewing glassy spots, has some orange scaling on the dorsal forewing, and a wider, more pronounced postmedian spot band on the ventral hindwing; Dun Skipper (pg. 127) lacks the prominent dorsal forewing glassy spots and has a uniformly dark-brown ventral hindwing or with just a very faint hint of a spot band

Comments: The Little Glassywing is named for the distinct translucent or glassy white spots on the forewing. It is a butterfly of shadier forest margins and adjacent moist habitats. While the adults readily visit flowers, they do not venture far into open areas and are seldom encountered in sunny gardens. Although widespread, populations tend to be fairly local. Males perch on low vegetation in sun-dappled locations to await passing females. The slender larvae construct individual tube-like leaf shelters on the host.

Little Glassywing

Pompeius verna

Family/Subfamily: Skippers (Hesperiidae)/
Grass-Skippers (Hesperiinae)

Wingspan: 1.0–1.5" (2.5–3.8 cm)

Above: dark brown; forewing in male has several small, transparent glassy spots, including one narrow, rectangular spot in
the center; forewing in female has several small transparent
glassy spots, including one square spot in the center

Below: hindwing is dark purplish brown with a faint postmedian
row of pale spots

Sexes: similar, although female's central glassy forewing spot is
noticeably square instead of rectangular

Egg: white, laid singly on host

Larva: green to greenish tan with fine white mottling, cream collar, and black head with two red spots on the lower margin

Larval Host Plants: various grasses, including Purpletop Tridens
(*Tridens flavus*)

Habitat: moist, open woodlands and clearings, forest margins,
wetlands, and adjacent semi-shaded habitats

Broods: one generation; larvea overwinter

Abundance: uncommon to common

Range: central and eastern portions of the region; uncommon
or absent westward and in the far north

Compare: Southern Broken-Dash (pg. 134) occurs only in extreme southern portions of the region and has an orange to reddish-brown ventral hindwing; Little Glassywing (pg. 129) has prominent dorsal forewing glassy spots and a less prominent ventral hindwing spot band; Dun Skipper (pg. 127) has a uniformly dark-brown ventral hindwing, possibly with just a very faint hint of a spot band

Comments: This widespread eastern skipper and the similar-looking Southern Broken-Dash were once considered the same species. Although called the Northern Broken-Dash, it ranges well into the Deep South into Florida and Texas, where the two species readily overlap. Its unique name comes from the black forewing stigma that is separated or "broken" into two distinct dashes. Adults are often found in open areas adjacent to wooded habitats and readily venture into nearby yards and gardens in search of nectar.

Northern Broken-Dash

Wallengrenia egeremet

Family/Subfamily: Skippers (Hesperiidae)/
   Grass-Skippers (Hesperiinae)

Wingspan: 1.0–1.5" (2.5–3.8 cm)

Above: dark brown; forewing in male has orange scaling along
   leading margin and a prominent black stigma divided
   into two parts and with a few small, orange postmedian
   spots; forewing in female is primarily dark brown with a
   few pale spots

Below: hindwing is dark purplish brown to slightly reddish
   brown with a curved postmedian row of pale spots

Sexes: dissimilar; female is primarily dark brown above with a
   few pale dorsal forewing spots and no black stigma

Egg: white, laid singly on host

Larva: brownish green with black head and cream collar

Larval Host Plants: various grasses, including panicgrass
   (*Panicum* spp.)

Habitat: open habitats, including forest margins and clearings,
   old fields, roadsides, utility easements, parks, and yards

Broods: one generation; larvae overwinter

Abundance: occasional to common

Range: central and eastern portions of the region; uncommon
   or absent westward

male

female

Compare: Fiery Skipper (pg. 233) has scattered small, dark spots on the ventral hindwing

Comments: The Sachem has an affinity for just about any open, sunny, and grassy habitats. A year-round resident of the Deep South, it regularly wanders northward to establish temporary colonies, especially across the southern half of our region. Farther north, it is considered a relatively rare stray. It is unable to survive harsh winter temperatures across the Midwest. Adults have a rapid, darting flight and are very fond of flowers. The larvae construct individual rolled leaf shelters on their hosts.

Sachem
Atalopedes campestris

Family/Subfamily: Skippers (Hesperiidae)/ Grass-Skippers (Hesperiinae)

Wingspan: 1.0–1.5" (2.5–3.8 cm)

Above: elongated wings; male is orange with dark-brown wing borders and a large, black forewing stigma; female is dark brown; hindwing has orange scaling in center; forewing has orange scaling at bases and along leading margin, with several semitransparent spots

Below: variable; hindwing is orange brown with a large central yellow-orange patch; female is brown with a postmedian band of cream spots and occasionally some orange scaling along leading margin of forewing

Sexes: dissimilar; female is darker with reduced orange and semitransparent dorsal forewing spots; ventral hindwing has a light postmedian spot band

Egg: cream, laid singly on host leaves

Larva: greenish brown with dark dorsal stripe and a black head

Larval Host Plants: various turf or weedy grasses, including crab-grass (*Digitaria* spp.) and Bermudagrass (*Cynodon dactylon*)

Habitat: open, disturbed sites, including roadsides, old fields, pastures, parks, yards, and gardens

Broods: one or more generations; does not overwinter in our region

Abundance: rare to occasional

Range: primarily southern portions of the region; rare or uncommon northward

Southern Broken-Dash
Wallengrenia otho

Family/Subfamily: Skippers (Hesperiidae)/
Grass-Skippers (Hesperiinae)

Wingspan: 1.0–1.5" (2.5–3.8 cm)

Habitat: woodlands and margins, wetlands, and roadsides

Range: extreme southern portions; rare to uncommon; localized

Sexes: dissimilar; dorsal forewing is brown in females, with pale dorsal forewing spots and no black stigma

Larva: gray brown with a dark dorsal stripe and black head

Above: dark brown; forewing in male has orange scaling along leading margin and a prominent black stigma divided into two parts and with a few small orange postmedian spots; forewing in female is dark brown with pale orange spots

Below: hindwing is reddish brown to tawny, especially in males, and with a faint curved spot band

Compare: Northern Broken-Dash (pg. 131)

Comments: Widespread throughout the Deep South, it barely extends into our region. It is often found alongside the similar-looking but darker Northern Broken-Dash.

Common Branded Skipper
Hesperia comma laurentina

Family/Subfamily: Skippers (Hesperiidae)/
Grass-Skippers (Hesperiinae)

Wingspan: 1.1–1.25" (2.8–3.2 cm)

Habitat: forests, roadsides, fields, and meadows

Range: extreme northern portions; uncommon to common; local

Sexes: dissimilar; female is darker above with reduced orange

Larva: dark greenish brown, often with mottling and a black head

Above: male is orange with wide, dark-brown wing borders and a black forewing stigma; female is brown; hindwing has an orange spot band; forewing has orange scaling along the leading margin and several pale orange to yellow spots

Below: hindwing is brownish orange with a greenish caste, an irregular white spot band, and two white basal spots

Compare: Leonard's Skipper (pg. 263)

Comments: This species has a wide global Holarctic distribution. Our subspecies, also called the Laurentian Skipper, occurs across northern portions of Michigan, Wisconsin, and Minnesota.

Compare: Sleepy Duskywing (pg. 159) is somewhat larger, flies earlier, and has a less prominent cell-end gray patch on the dorsal forewing

Comments: The Dreamy Duskywing is an early-season species widespread across Canada, the Mountain West, Appalachians, and the Northeast. In our region, it is most frequently encountered across the Upper Great Lakes south into Ohio and Indiana. Adults lack the glassy forewing spots common in most other members of the genus *Erynnis*. Males scurry low to the ground among vegetation and regularly perch on bare twigs or in sunlit patches on the ground to await passing females. They also regularly puddle at damp soil. Larvae construct individual leaf shelters on the host.

Dreamy Duskywing
Erynnis icelus

Family/Subfamily: Skippers (Hesperiidae)/
Spread-Wing Skippers (Pyrginae)

Wingspan: 1.0–1.6" (2.5–4.1 cm)

Above: dark brown; forewing has extensive gray scaling on outer
half and two black, chain-like bands enclosing a broad gray
patch at the end of the cell; lacks glassy spots; hindwing has
two rows of pale spots; labial palpi are noticeably long and
project forward

Below: dark brown; hindwing has two rows of light spots

Sexes: similar, although females are lighter and more
heavily patterned

Egg: green turning reddish, laid singly on the host twigs
or leaves

Larva: light green with a dark dorsal stripe and white lateral
stripes and covered in small white dots; head is brown with
orange spots around the margin

Larval Host Plants: primarily willows (*Salix* spp.) and poplars and
aspens (*Populus* spp.); locust (*Robinia* spp.) and birch (*Betula*
spp.) may also be used

Habitat: open woodlands, margins and adjacent clearings,
brushy areas, and moist woodland depressions

Broods: one generation; larvae overwinter

Abundance: rare to common

Range: primarily northern and eastern portions of the region

Cobweb Skipper
Hesperia metea

Family/Subfamily: Skippers (Hesperiidae)/
Grass-Skippers (Hesperiinae)

Wingspan: 1.1–1.4" (2.8–3.6 cm)

Habitat: savanna, prairie, barrens, and adjacent open areas

Range: scattered throughout eastern and southern portions of
the region; rare to uncommon; localized

Sexes: dissimilar; dorsal forewing is brown in females with pale
dorsal forewing spots and no black stigma

Larva: gray brown with a dark dorsal stripe and round black head

Above: male is tawny orange; forewing has broad brown borders,
pale spots, and a black stigma; female is brown; forewing has
small white spots

Below: hindwing is olive brown with irregular white band and
spots; white scaling gives a somewhat cobweb appearance

Compare: unique

Comments: Highly localized populations are imperiled throughout our region. Larvae feed on Little Bluestem (*Schizachyrium
scoparium*) and Big Bluestem (*Andropogon gerardi*).

Linda's Roadside-Skipper
Amblyscirtes linda

Family/Subfamily: Skippers (Hesperiidae)/
  Grass-Skippers (Hesperiinae)

Wingspan: 1.1–1.3" (2.8–3.3 cm)

Habitat: moist hardwood forests and stream margins

Range: southern Illinois, Missouri, and eastern Kansas; rare; local

Sexes: similar

Larva: blue green with a white head marked by brown

Above: dull dark brown; forewing has white subapical spots

Below: hindwing is dark brown with scattered white scaling,
  noticeably more frosted toward the outer margin, with a
  band (often faint) of central white spots; wing fringes are
  checkered; forewing has small, white subapical spots

Compare: Pepper and Salt Skipper (pg. 91), Bell's Roadside-
  Skipper (pg. 112), and Common Roadside-Skipper (pg. 109)

Comments: An endemic species in the Ozark and Ouachita
  Mountains in the lower Midwest. Populations tend to be small,
  highly localized, and of conservation concern. Larvae utilize
  Indian Woodoats (*Chasmanthium latifolium*) as a larval host.

Compare: unique

Comments: Often called the Inornate Ringlet, this pretty little butterfly is our smallest satyr. Numerous subspecies are found from Newfoundland to British Columbia and south to southern California and West Virginia. The butterfly appears to be increasing in many locations. Unlike most members of the subfamily, the adults readily visit flowers. They have a slow, bobbing flight and maneuver low over grassy vegetation.

Common Ringlet
Coenonympha tullia

Family/Subfamily: Brush-Footed Butterflies (Nymphalidae)/ Satyrs and Wood-Nymphs (Satyrinae)

Wingspan: 1.1–1.5" (2.8–3.8 cm)

Above: unmarked orange brown

Below: forewing is orange brown toward the base; outer margin is gray and typically has a small, pale-rimmed black eyespot toward the apex; hindwing is grayish brown and somewhat two-toned; both wings have an irregular, whitish median band (often incomplete on the hindwing)

Sexes: similar, although the female has somewhat broader wings and increased orange scaling above

Egg: yellowish, round, laid singly on host leaves

Larva: green with a yellow lateral stripe and two short, pink-tipped tails

Larval Host Plants: various grasses

Habitat: variety of open, grassy landscapes, open woodlands and margins, fields, roadsides, and meadows

Broods: one generation; larvae overwinter

Abundance: occasional to abundant; local

Range: northern third of the region

Compare: Northern Cloudywing (pg. 147) has smaller, glassy white forewing spots, glassy white apical spots that form a misaligned band, and a darker face

Comments: Although called the Southern Cloudywing, the range of this dull-brown skipper extends well into the Midwest and even southern Ontario. In portions of our region, it is often found alongside the similar-looking and more widespread Northern Cloudywing, making quick identification a bit more challenging. Adults perch on the ground or on low vegetation, typically with their wings partially open. They are often wary and difficult to closely approach. The larvae construct individual leaf shelters on the host.

Southern Cloudywing

Thorybes bathyllus

Family/Subfamily: Skippers (Hesperiidae)/
Dicot Skippers (Eudaminae)

Wingspan: 1.2–1.6" (3.0–4.1 cm)

Above: brown; forewing has several small, glassy white subapical spots forming a straight band and a postmedian band of
larger glassy white spots; wing fringes are checkered; forewing
in male lacks a costal fold

Below: brown; hindwing is darker toward base, with two wavy,
dark parallel bands; both wings have lavender gray scaling
along margin; light face

Sexes: similar

Egg: light green, laid singly on host leaves

Larva: light green to greenish brown with thin, dark dorsal stripe
and narrow, pale lateral stripe; bulbous black head; body is
covered with numerous short, light-colored hairs

Larval Host Plants: various pea family (*Fabaceae*) plants,
including American Hogpeanut (*Amphicarpaea bracteata*),
lespedeza (*Lespedeza* spp.), tick-trefoil (*Desmodium* spp.),
Atlantic Pigeonwings (*Clitoria mariana*), and milkvetch
(*Astragulus* spp),

Habitat: open woodlands and margins; brush fields; roadsides;
old fields; and other dry, open areas

Broods: one generation; larvae overwinter

Abundance: occasional to common

Range: southern half of the region

Columbine Duskywing
Erynnis lucilius

Family/Subfamily: Skippers (Hesperiidae)/
Spread-Wing Skippers (Pyrginae)

Wingspan: 1.2–1.6" (3.0–4.1 cm)

Habitat: woodlands and margins; ravines

Range: primarily Upper Great Lakes; uncommon to rare; localized

Sexes: similar, although female is more heavily patterned

Larva: pale green with tiny white spots, dark dorsal stripe,
narrow lateral cream stripes, and a black head

Above: dark brown; forewing has black, brown, and light-brown
pattern elements and several small, glassy subapical spots;
females have increased gray forewing scaling

Below: dark brown; hindwing with rows of pale spots

Compare: Wild Indigo Duskywing (pg. 157)

Comments: Generally uncommon with scattered populations.
Habitat preference may help distinguish it from other duskywings. Larvae utilize Red Columbine (*Aquilegia canadensis*)
as sole host.

Mottled Duskywing
Erynnis martialis

Family/Subfamily: Skippers (Hesperiidae)/
Spread-Wing Skippers (Pyrginae)

Wingspan: 1.2–1.6" (3.0–4.1 cm)

Habitat: open woodlands, forest margins, and barrens

Range: scattered throughout several states; uncommon to rare

Sexes: similar, although female has increased gray scaling on
forewing and is more heavily patterned

Larva: pale green with tiny white spots, narrow lateral cream
stripes, and a black head marked with orange spots around
the margin

Above: brown; strongly patterned with black, brown, and light
brown, giving overall mottled appearance; forewing has
several small, glassy subapical spots; females have more-
gray forewing scaling; fresh individuals have violet sheen

Below: brown with numerous light and dark spots

Compare: Wild Indigo Duskywing (pg. 157)

Comments: Widely distributed but very fragmented. Localized
populations are declining to imperiled in many locations.

Compare: Southern Cloudywing (pg. 143) has larger, glassy white forewing spots, glassy white subapical spots that form an aligned band, and a lighter face

Comments: Widespread from the Deep South to central Canada, the Northern Cloudywing essentially replaces the similar-looking Southern Cloudwing in the northern half of the region. When they do fly together, close examination is required to reliably separate the two species. Adults have a low, skipping flight and scurry quickly along trails and clearings, pausing occasionally to sip nectar from available flowers. Males perch on the ground or on low vegetation and aggressively dart out to engage rivals. Larvae construct individual leaf shelters on the host.

Northern Cloudywing

Thorybes pylades

Family/Subfamily: Skippers (Hesperiidae)/
Dicot Skippers (Eudaminae)

Wingspan: 1.2–1.7" (3.0–4.3 cm)

Above: brown; forewing has several small, misaligned, glassy white subapical spots; wing fringes are checkered; forewing in male has a costal fold

Below: brown; hindwing is darker towards base with two parallel, wavy dark bands; both wings have lavender-gray scaling along margin, more pronounced on hindwing; dark face

Sexes: similar

Egg: light green, laid singly on the undersides of host leaves

Larva: light green to greenish brown with thin, dark dorsal stripe and narrow, pale lateral stripe; has a bulbous black head; body is covered with numerous short, light-colored hairs

Larval Host Plants: various pea family (*Fabaceae*) plants, including American Hogpeanut (*Amphicarpaea bracteata*), lespedeza (*Lespedeza* spp.), Atlantic Pigeonwings (*Clitoria mariana*), Groundnut (*Apios americana*), and tick-trefoil (*Desmodium* spp.)

Habitat: open woodlands and margins; brush fields; roadsides; old fields; and other dry, open areas

Broods: one generation; larvae overwinter

Abundance: occasional to common

Range: throughout

Two-Spotted Skipper
Euphyes bimacula

Family/Subfamily: Skippers (Hesperiidae)/
Grass-Skippers (Hesperiinae)

Wingspan: 1.25–1.4" (3.2–3.6 cm)

Habitat: wet meadows, fens, and marshes; moist roadsides

Range: primarily central portions; rare to uncommon; local

Sexes: dissimilar; female is primarily dark brown with two pale
dorsal forewing spots and no stigma

Larva: green with white mottling; brown head is marked with
cream lines, a black oval on the top, and a black collar

Above: dark-brown wings; head and thorax are orange on top;
forewing in male has tawny orange scaling along basal portion of leading margin and around black stigma

Below: hindwing is an unmarked orange brown with lighter
veins and distinctive white fringe along the inner margin;
body appears two-toned orange brown above, lighter below

Compare: unique

Comments: Poorly known specialist of sedge-dominated wetlands. It is generally of conservation concern throughout.

Persius Duskywing
Erynnis persius

Family/Subfamily: Skippers (Hesperiidae)/
Spread-Wing Skippers (Pyrginae)

Wingspan: 1.25–1.7" (3.2–4.3 cm)

Habitat: open woodlands, pine-oak barrens, and fields

Range: central portions; rare to occasional; local

Sexes: similar, although female is lighter with more heavily patterned wings and larger forewing spots

Larva: light green with a dark dorsal stripe and white lateral stripes, and covered in small white dots; head is dark brown

Above: dark brown; forewing has darker brownish-black spot bands and gray scaling; has an aligned postmedian row of small glassy spots and a gray patch at the end of the cell; hindwing is brown with faint light spots along outer margin

Below: dark brown; hindwing has two rows of light spots

Compare: Wild Indigo (pg. 157), Columbine (pg. 144), and Horace's Duskywing (pg. 153)

Comments: A species of conservation concern. Adults have a quick, bouncing flight and fly low among plants.

Compare: Dion Skipper (pg. 167) is larger and has two long, pale rays through the ventral hindwing without any adjacent post-median spots

Comments: Generally an uncommon butterfly throughout its limited midwestern range, the Black Dash is restricted to wetlands where its host sedges grow. As a result, populations tend to be highly fragmented and small. It may often be found alongside other wetland specialist species, including Mulberry Wing, Broad-Winged Skipper, and Long Dash. The adults are swift on the wing but easily observed when feeding at flowers. They are particularly fond of milkweeds.

Black Dash
Euphyes conspicua

Family/Subfamily: Skippers (Hesperiidae)/
Grass-Skippers (Hesperiinae)

Wingspan: 1.25–1.6" (3.2–4.1 cm)

Above: male is golden orange with broad, dark-brown wing borders and a thick black stigma; female is dark brown; forewing
has a band of cream-yellow spots

Below: hindwing is orange brown to reddish brown, with a large
and somewhat diffuse yellow median patch that is widest in
the middle

Sexes: dissimilar; female is primarily dark brown with pale forewing spots

Egg: white, laid singly on host

Larva: green with fine white mottling; brown head marked with
cream lines around the margin and a black oval on the top

Larval Host Plants: various sedges, including Upright Sedge (*Carex
stricta*) and Eastern Narrowleaf Sedge (*Carex amphibola*)

Habitat: freshwater wetlands, including fens, marshes, sedge
meadows, roadside ditches, and stream margins

Broods: one generation; larvae overwinter

Abundance: uncommon to occasional; local

Range: primarily northeast portion of the region

Compare: Juvenal's Duskywing (pg. 173) has increased gray scaling on the dorsal forewing, larger glassy forewing spots, and two pale spots along the leading margin on the ventral hindwing; overall darker, more black-looking above

Comments: Although widespread throughout much of the East, Horace's Duskywing becomes less common northward into the Upper Midwest. A butterfly of wooded habitats with an abundance of oaks, it often wanders into adjacent, more-open, disturbed sites in search of nectar. As a result, the species can be a frequent visitor to gardens and forested yards. It tends to be on the wing later than the similar-looking, spring-flying Juvenal's Duskywing. Adults have a quick, somewhat erratic flight and perch and feed with wings outstretched. Males often visit damp earth with some regularity. Larvae construct individual leaf shelters on the host.

Horace's Duskywing

Erynnis horatius

Family/Subfamily: Skippers (Hesperiidae)/
Spread-Wing Skippers (Pyrginae)

Wingspan: 1.25–1.75" (3.2–4.4 cm)

Above: dark brown; forewing is patterned with brown, gray, and
black; has postmedian row of small glassy spots; hindwing
has two rows of pale spots

Below: as above but paler

Sexes: similar, although female is more heavily patterned,
has increased gray scaling on forewing and larger glassy
forewing spots

Egg: pale green, laid singly on young host leaves

Larva: light green with a pale lateral stripe and covered in
small white dots; head is brown with orange spots around
the margin

Larval Host Plants: various oaks (*Quercus* spp.), including Post
Oak (*Quercus stellata*), Water Oak (*Quercus nigra*), and
Black Oak (*Quercus velutina*)

Habitat: woodlands, margins and adjacent clearings, roadsides,
and brushy areas; also forested parks and neighborhoods

Broods: two generations; larvae overwinter

Abundance: rare to occasional

Range: southern portions of the region

Dukes' Skipper
Euphyes dukesi

Family/Subfamily: Skippers (Hesperiidae)/
Grass-Skippers (Hesperiinae)

Wingspan: 1.3–1.6" (3.6–4.1 cm)

Habitat: wooded swamps and marshes

Range: southeastern parts of the region; rare to uncommon; local

Sexes: similar, but female has pale yellow dorsal forewing spots

Larva: green with fine white mottling; brown head is marked with cream lines around the margin, a black oval on the top, and a black collar

Above: rounded wings; male is a blackish brown with faint tawny-orange scaling and at the base of the leading margin, and a black stigma; hindwing is orange with broad blackish-brown borders; forewing in female has two small, pale central spots

Below: hindwing is orange brown with two yellow rays

Compare: other Skippers (pgs. 167, 127, and 169)

Comments: Adults maneuver low among vegetation and can be easily overlooked. Generally of conservation concern.

Mitchell's Satyr
Neonympha mitchellii

Family/Subfamily: Brush Footed Butterflies (Nymphalidae)/ Satyrs and Wood-Nymphs (Satyrinae)

Wingspan: 1.3–1.9" (3.3–4.8 cm)

Habitat: prairie fens

Range: southern Michigan and northern Indiana; occasional to abundant; local

Sexes: similar

Larva: bluish green with lighter lateral stripes and two short tails; one generation; larvae overwinter

Above: uniform, unmarked brown

Below: brown; hindwing has a submarginal row of somewhat oval (or irregularly shaped), yellow-rimmed black eyespots with silver highlights, surrounded by orange-brown band; forewing also has some smaller eyespots

Compare: Little Wood Satyr (pg. 175)

Comments: Due to habitat loss and alteration, it is critically imperiled and federally listed as endangered.

Compare: Horace's Duskywing (pg. 153) is generally larger and lighter brown on inner half of the dorsal forewing; Juvenal's Duskywing (pg. 173) is larger and has two pale spots along the leading margin of the dorsal hindwing; Columbine Duskywing (pg. 144) is somewhat smaller and is associated with wooded habitats supporting patches of its host

Comments: Named for one of its primary larval hosts, the Wild Indigo Duskywing occurs throughout much of the eastern US and southern Ontario. It has become more widespread because of its ability to colonize and utilize Crownvetch, a nonnative ground cover and cover crop that is often used along roadsides to help stabilize soils. Adults have a low, somewhat erratic flight but readily pause to nectar or perch on sunlit vegetation. Careful observation is needed to reliably separate this species from other duskywings. Larvae construct individual leaf shelters with silk.

Wild Indigo Duskywing
Erynnis baptisiae

Family/Subfamily: Skippers (Hesperiidae)/
Spread-Wing Skippers (Pyrginae)

Wingspan: 1.3–1.7" (3.3–4.3 cm)

Above: dark brown; forewing has a darker base and a prominent
lighter gray-brown cell-end patch outwardly bordered by
band of darker, often triangular spots enclosing several small,
glassy subapical spots

Below: as above with faint paler spots

Sexes: similar, although female has somewhat larger white
forewing spots

Egg: green, laid singly on host leaves, becoming pink with age

Larva: light green with a pale lateral stripe and covered in
tiny white dots; dark brown to black often with orange dots
around the margin

Larval Host Plants: various pea family (Fabaceae) plants, including
wild indigo (*Baptisia* spp.) and Crownvetch (*Securigera varia*)

Habitat: open, disturbed sites, including roadsides, weedy fields,
and utility easements; also forest margins

Broods: two generations; larvae overwinter

Abundance: occasional

Range: southern two-thirds of the region; rare or absent northward and far western portions

Compare: Dreamy Duskywing (pg. 137) is somewhat smaller, flies later, and has a prominent cell-end gray patch on the dorsal forewing

Comments: The Sleepy Duskywing typically starts its spring flight earlier than the similar-looking but smaller Dreamy Duskywing. It also has an affinity for xeric habitats where host oaks abound. Together, they are the only two members of the genus *Erynnis* that lack the often-conspicuous small, glassy forewing spots. As a result, they often present a considerable challenge to separate in the field. Careful observation is often needed to render an accurate identification. Adults perch and feed with their wings held open, a common behavior of duskywings. Larvae construct individual leaf shelters on the host.

Sleepy Duskywing

Erynnis brizo

Family/Subfamily: Skippers (Hesperiidae)/
Spread-Wing Skippers (Pyrginae)

Wingspan: 1.3–1.75" (3.3–4.4 cm)

Above: dark brown; forewing has extensive gray scaling on outer
half and two black, chain-like bands; lacks glassy spots; hindwing has two rows of pale spots; labial palpi are noticeably
long and project forward

Below: dark brown; hindwing has two rows of light spots

Sexes: similar, although female is lighter and more
heavily patterned

Egg: green, laid singly on host leaves

Larva: light green with a pale lateral stripe and covered in small
white dots; head is brown with orange spots around margin

Larval Host Plants: various oaks (*Quercus* spp.), including Black
Oak (*Quercus velutina*)

Habitat: dry open woodlands, margins and adjacent clearings,
brushy areas, and barrens

Broods: one generation; larvae overwinter

Abundance: rare to common; local

Range: primarily eastern and southern portions of the region

Compare: Taiga Alpine (pg. 163) has row of four black eyespots surrounded by orange on the dorsal forewing; reported only from northern Minnesota

Comments: The Red-Disked Alpine is a widespread boreal species that is more common in western portions of its range. Its range extends into our region across the extreme northern portion of the Upper Great Lakes. The fairly plain-looking adults lack eyespots but boast a lovely chestnut-colored forewing patch for which the species is named. They have a weak flight and maneuver close to the ground, perching regularly on low grasses or bare ground. It remains a poorly known butterfly.

Red-Disked Alpine

Erebia discoidalis

Family/Subfamily: Brush-Footed Butterflies (Nymphalidae)/ Satyrs and Wood-Nymphs (Satyrinae)

Wingspan: 1.34–1.77" (3.4–4.5 cm)

Above: dark brown; forewing has a large, central reddish-brown patch

Below: dark brown; forewing is reddish brown toward base; hindwing is striated with light grayish-white frosting (scaling) toward the outer margin

Sexes: similar

Egg: not reported

Larva: cream with darker diagonal marks

Larval Host Plants: bluegrass (*Poa* spp.)

Habitat: grassy bogs and margins, grassy meadows, forest glades, and ridgetops

Broods: one generation; larvae overwinter; possibly biennial

Abundance: rare to uncommon; local

Range: northern Minnesota, Wisconsin, and Michigan

Compare: Red-Disked Alpine (pg. 161) lacks forewing eyespots

Comments: This is another widespread boreal alpine that just barely extends southward into our region in northeastern Minnesota. Its preference for open forested bogs adds to its spotty, highly localized occurrence. Relatively little is known of the Taiga Alpine's life history and ecology. Adults rarely visit flowers but can be seen at damp ground and likely feed on sap flows, animal waste, and carrion. Due to is restricted distribution in our region, all known populations should be conserved.

Taiga Alpine
Erebia mancinus

Family/Subfamily: Brush-Footed Butterflies (Nymphalidae)/
Satyrs and Wood-Nymphs (Satyrinae)

Wingspan: 1.35–1.77" (3.5–4.5 cm)

Above: dark brown; forewing center is reddish brown with a
submarginal row of black eyespots in an orange field

Below: forewing as above; hindwing is mottled dark brown with
some light-gray scaling toward the outer margin

Sexes: similar

Egg: unknown

Larva: unknown

Larval Host Plants: unknown, likely grasses or sedges

Habitat: open Black Spruce bogs

Broods: one generation; larvae likely overwinter

Abundance: rare; local

Range: northern Minnesota

Compare: Zabulon Skipper (pg. 123) male has a ventral hindwing spot band with scattered small dark spots; female has a ventral hindwing with extensive purple-gray frosting and a white bar along the upper angle

Comments: This small woodland skipper has a single late-spring to early-summer flight. Males perch on sunlit leaves along trails and margins and aggressively dart out to investigate passing butterflies or other insects. Although preferring shadier conditions, both sexes readily venture into nearby open areas in search of nectar. Hobomok Skippers are replaced southward by the similar-looking Zabulon Skipper. The two fly together in some locations. Larvae construct individual leaf shelters on the host.

Hobomok Skipper
Poanes hobomok

Family/Subfamily: Skippers (Hesperiidae)/
Grass-Skippers (Hesperiinae)

Wingspan: 1.4–1.6" (3.6–4.12 cm)

Above: male is bright orange with broad, dark-brown wing borders; forewing has a thin, dark cell-end bar; female has two forms: normal form resembles male but has reduced orange scaling; form 'Pocahontas' is primarily dark brown with a few pale yellow-orange forewing spots

Below: hindwing is dark brown with a broad, yellow-orange spot band in the center; the elongated centermost spot extends well past the others toward the outer margin; hindwing border has purplish-gray frosting; hindwing in female form 'Pocahontas' is dark purplish brown with a faint light spot band

Sexes: dissimilar; female Hobomoks have two forms, both darker than the male

Egg: white, laid singly on host

Larva: brown green to pinkish brown with tiny white spots and a dark brown head; overall velvety appearance

Larval Host Plants: various grasses, including Little Bluestem (*Schizachyrium scoparium*), orchardgrass (*Dactylis* spp.), and panicgrass (*Panicum* spp.)

Habitat: open woodlands; forest margins; and adjacent trails, roadsides, and open areas

Broods: one generation; larvae and pupae overwinter

Abundance: uncommon to common

Range: generally throughout; most common in northeastern portions; less common south and west

Compare: Dukes' Skipper (pg. 154) lacks bright-orange scaling above, has rounder wings, and prefers shadier wetlands; Black Dash (pg. 151) is smaller and has a yellow ventral hindwing patch instead of long rays

Comments: Another large, dark skipper of wetland habitats, the Dion Skipper has richly colored ventral hindwings with distinctive (albeit often faint) long, pale rays that run along the veins almost the entire length of the wing. Throughout much of its irregular eastern range, the species is quite localized and seldom numerous. Nonetheless, it can often be reliably encountered in most suitable habitat areas. Adults are sluggish fliers and seldom venture far from their wetland habitats. Larvae construct individual rolled leaf shelters on their hosts.

Dion Skipper
Euphyes dion

Family/Subfamily: Skippers (Hesperiidae)/
Grass-Skippers (Hesperiinae)

Wingspan: 1.4–1.7" (3.3–4.3 cm)

Above: male is golden orange with broad, dark-brown wing borders and a thick black stigma; female is dark brown; forewing has a band of light-orange spots

Below: hindwing is orange brown to reddish brown with two long, pale, and often-faint rays, including a more prominent one through the center

Sexes: dissimilar; female is primarily dark brown with pale forewing spots

Egg: white, laid singly on host

Larva: green with fine white mottling; brown head is marked with cream lines around the margin, a black oval on the top, and a black collar

Larval Host Plants: various sedges, including Hairy Sedge (*Carex lacustris*) and Shoreline Sedge (*Scirpus cyperinus*); possibly also Woolgrass (*Scirpus cyperinus*)

Habitat: freshwater wetlands, including fens, marshes, sedge meadows, roadside ditches, and stream margins

Broods: one generation; larvae overwinter

Abundance: uncommon to occasional; local

Range: throughout; rare or absent in far western portions of the region

Dusted Skipper

Atrytonopsis hianna

Family/Subfamily: Skippers (Hesperiidae)/
Grass-Skippers (Hesperiinae)

Wingspan: 1.4–1.7" (3.6–4.3 cm)

Habitat: dry habitats, including prairies, barrens, old fields, and
utility easements

Range: throughout; rare to uncommon; local

Sexes: similar, although female has larger forewing spots

Larva: gray, pinkish dorsally, with long cream hairs giving an
overall fuzzy appearance, a brown anal segment, and a
purple-brown unmarked head

Above: dark chocolate brown with several small white forewing
spots; noticeable white line for each eye

Below: hindwing is dark chocolate brown with purple-gray frosting on outer portion and one or more small basal white spots

Compare: unique

Comments: Populations are imperiled or of conservation concern virtually throughout. Requires early successional habitat
maintained by active management such as fire.

Broad-Winged Skipper
Poanes viator

Family/Subfamily: Skippers (Hesperiidae)/
Grass-Skippers (Hesperiinae)

Wingspan: 1.4–2.0" (3.6–5.0 cm)

Habitat: freshwater wetlands, sedge meadows, and marshes

Range: primarily Upper Great Lakes; also extreme southern
portions; uncommon to occasional; local

Sexes: similar, but female has pale yellow dorsal forewing spots

Larva: pale brown with a velvety appearance and pale head

Above: broad wings; hindwing is orange with a broad, dark-
brown border; forewing is dark brown with some orange
scaling along leading margin and orange spots in male or
pale yellow in female; male lacks black stigma

Below: hindwing is tawny brown with a distinct long, golden
ray through a central spot band, leaving one spot above
the ray and the rest below

Compare: Dion Skipper (pg. 167)

Comments: A large, robust wetland specialist. Larvae feed on various sedges, reeds, and Northern Wild Rice (*Zizania plustris*).

Compare: Silver-Spotted Skipper (pg. 191) is larger, has elongated forewings, and has a clear white ventral hindwing patch; Golden-Banded Skipper (pg. 176) lacks ventral white patch on hindwing margin

Comments: This attractive skipper is named for the prominent grayish-white (hoary) patch on the ventral hindwing margin. This field mark is easily seen when adults are feeding from flowers. Primarily a butterfly of dry, sunny woodland margins and nearby open areas, populations tend to be somewhat localized. The Hoary Edge is seldom numerous and is most often encountered as lone individuals. Males are territorial and readily fly out to investigate passing insects before returning to their perch soon afterwards. The larvae construct individual leaf shelters on the host.

Hoary Edge

Achalarus lyciades

Family/Subfamily: Skippers (Hesperiidae)/
Dicot Skippers (Eudaminae)

Wingspan: 1.4–1.75" (3.6–4.4 cm)

Above: brown; forewing has median band of gold spots; wing
fringes are checkered

Below: forewing as above but muted; hindwing is mottled dark
brown with a distinct dirty-white marginal patch

Sexes: similar

Egg: cream, laid singly on host leaves

Larva: light green to pinkish brown with dark dorsal stripe and
an orange lateral stripe; covered in small yellow dots; head is
an unmarked black

Larval Host Plants: tick-trefoil (*Desmodium* spp.); lespedeza
(*Lespedeza* spp.) may also be used

Habitat: open woodlands and margins; brush fields; and
adjacent roadsides, meadows, and clearings

Broods: two generations; pupae overwinter

Abundance: uncommon to occasional

Range: southern portions of the region

Compare: Horace's Duskywing (pg. 153) has less gray scaling on the dorsal forewing, has smaller glassy forewing spots, and lacks the two pale spots along the leading margin on the ventral hindwing

Comments: Widespread across much of the eastern US and southern Canada, Juvenal's Duskywing is a relatively common early-season species that can at times be quite abundant. It is one of several very similar-looking duskywings that can pose a challenge to identify reliably in the field. Careful observation is often needed. Older, worn individuals may be nearly impossible to determine. Adults have quick, erratic flight and readily stop at available blooms. Primarily a butterfly of forests and adjacent open areas with oaks.

Juvenal's Duskywing
Erynnis juvenalis

Family/Subfamily: Skippers (Hesperiidae)/
Spread-Wing Skippers (Pyrginae)

Wingspan: 1.5–1.9" (3.8–4.8 cm)

Above: dark brown; forewing is heavily patterned with brown, gray, and black; has a postmedian row of small glassy spots and one inside the cell; hindwing has two rows of pale spots

Below: forewing is marked as above but paler; hindwing has two pale spots along the leading margin

Sexes: similar, although female is more heavily patterned, has increased gray scaling on forewing and larger glassy forewing spots

Egg: pale green, laid singly on young host leaves

Larva: light green with a pale lateral stripe and covered in small white dots; head is brown with orange spots around margin

Larval Host Plants: various oaks (*Quercus* spp.), including Post Oak (*Quercus stellata*), White Oak (*Quercus alba*), and Black Oak (*Quercus velutina*)

Habitat: woodlands, margins and adjacent clearings, roadsides, and brushy areas; also forested parks and neighborhoods

Broods: one generation; larvae overwinter

Abundance: occasional to abundant

Range: all but western portions of the region, where it is absent or uncommon

ventral

Compare: Mitchell's Satyr (pg. 155) is restricted to only a few small populations in southern Michigan and Indiana; has oval (or irregularly shaped) eyespots

Comments: This plain brown butterfly is widespread and generally common throughout the Midwest. A butterfly of shady woodland habitats, it dances along the forest floor with a low, bobbing flight. Adults frequently perch on leaf litter or low vegetation in light gaps with their wings partially open. Late-instar larvae overwinter and complete development the following spring.

Little Wood Satyr

Megisto cymela

Family/Subfamily: Brush-Footed Butterflies (Nymphalidae)/
Satyrs and Wood-Nymphs (Satyrinae)

Wingspan: 1.5–1.9" (3.3–4.8 cm)

Above: brown; forewing has two yellow-rimmed black eyespots;
hindwing has one to three (usually one is quite small)
yellow-rimmed black eyespots

Below: brown with two dark lines through the middle of both
wings; each wing has some pearly silver marks between two
large, yellow-rimmed black eyespots

Sexes: similar, although female has larger eyespots

Egg: green, round, laid singly on host leaves

Larva: brown with a dark dorsal stripe; brown lateral dashes;
two short, stubby tails; and two small horns off the head

Larval Host Plants: various grasses, including Orchardgrass
(*Dactylis glomerata*) and Kentucky Bluegrass (*Poa pratensis*)

Habitat: open woodlands, forest clearings, fens, woodland
margins, and adjacent brushy areas

Broods: one generation; larvae overwinter

Abundance: occasional to abundant; local

Range: throughout, although less common in far western
portions of the region

Golden-Banded Skipper
Autochton cellus

Family/Subfamily: Skippers (Hesperiidae)/
Spread-Wing Skippers (Pyrginae)

Wingspan: 1.5–2.0" (3.8–5.1 cm)

Habitat: woodlands, fields, and roadsides

Range: southern portions; uncommon to occasional

Sexes: similar

Larva: light green to pinkish brown with dark dorsal stripe and
an orange lateral stripe; covered in small yellow dots; head
unmarked black

Above: brown; forewing has a translucent golden-yellow median
spot band and a white apical spot; checkered wing fringes

Below: forewing as above but muted; hindwing is mottled dark
brown often with gray-white marginal scaling

Compare: Silver-Spotted Skipper (pg. 191)

Comments: Named for the prominent translucent golden band
through the forewing. Males are territorial and readily fly out
to investigate passing insects. The larvae construct individual
leaf shelters on the host.

Long-Tailed Skipper
Urbanus proteus

Family/Subfamily: Skippers (Hesperiidae)/
Dicot Skippers (Eudaminae)

Wingspan: 1.5–2.0" (3.8–5.1 cm)

Habitat: open disturbed sites, forest margins, and gardens

Range: primarily extreme southern portions; stray northward

Sexes: similar

Larva: yellow green with a dark dorsal stripe, yellow lateral
stripes, and a bulbous crimson head with two red dots along
the lower margin; body covered in small black spots

Above: brown with iridescent blue-green scaling on wing bases
and body; long hindwing tail; forewing is elongated, with
several transparent glassy spots

Below: brown; hindwing has two prominent dark brown bands;
forewing has continuous brown submarginal band

Compare: unique

Comments: It establishes temporary breeding colonies northward. Resulting adults migrate south each fall to overwinter.
Larvae use various pea family (Fabaceae) plants as hosts.

177

Compare: unique

Comments: The Common Buckeye is one of our most distinctive species and unlikely to be confused with any other butterfly. The prominent eyespots help deflect attacks away from the insect's vulnerable body or serve to startle would-be predators. It is a seasonal immigrant that temporarily colonizes our area but cannot survive the cold winters. As a result, they migrate in the fall to the Deep South and overwinter as adults. Continued climate warming has accelerated the timing and northward range expansion of this butterfly. Adults have a strong, low flight and are very wary of close approach.

Common Buckeye
Junonia coenia

Family/Subfamily: Brush-Footed Butterflies (Nymphalidae)/ True Brush-Foots (Nymphalinae)

Wingspan: 1.5–2.4" (3.8–6.1 cm)

Above: brown with prominent target-shaped eyespots on both wings; forewing has distinct white postmedian band and two orange cell bars

Below: forewing as above only somewhat muted; hindwing is seasonally variable; summer forms are light brown with numerous pattern elements; cool-season forms are reddish brown with reduced markings; both forms somewhat resemble a dead leaf

Sexes: similar, although female has broader wings and larger hindwing eyespots

Egg: small, green, laid singly on host leaves

Larva: black with lateral cream-white stripes, orange patches, blue spots, and numerous black, branched spines; lateral spines have orange bases

Larval Host Plants: numerous herbaceous plants in several families (Acanthaceae, Verbenaceae, Scrophulariaceae, and Plantaginaceae), including toadflax (*Nuttallanthus* spp.), false foxglove (*Agalinis* spp.), and plantain (*Plantago* spp.)

Habitat: old fields, pastures, roadsides, fallow agricultural land, easements, gardens and yards, and disturbed sites

Broods: one to several generations; adults overwinter

Abundance: rare to common

Range: throughout, although occasional to absent farther north and west

Compare: Jutta Arctic (pg. 187) is less boldly patterned on the ventral hindwing, lacks white veins, and is found in bogs; Macoun's Arctic (pg. 183) is less boldly patterned below and lacks white veins

Comments: Although widespread throughout the Mountain West, the Chryxus Arctic has a much more limited eastern range. It can be found in northern Michigan, Wisconsin, and eastern Canada. It is found in dry habitats. Its populations tend to be rather local, but adults can be fairly common when encountered. Flying quickly over open ground and low vegetation, individuals can present quite a challenge to follow or catch.

Chryxus Arctic

Oeneis chryxus

Family/Subfamily: Brush-Footed Butterflies (Nymphalidae)/ Satyrs and Wood-Nymphs (Satyrinae)

Wingspan: 1.6–2.1" (4.1–5.3 cm)

Above: light orange brown with darker margins; forewing has a submarginal row of two to four black eyespots; male forewing has darkened gray scent scales along leading edge; hindwing has a small black eyespot at anal angle

Below: forewing as above with dark postmedian line having a sharp, outward pointing tooth; hindwing is mottled brown and gray with heavy striations and white veins

Sexes: similar

Egg: cream, laid singly near host

Larva: light brown with darker brown and cream lateral strips

Larval Host Plants: various grasses, including Poverty Oatgrass (*Danthonia spicata*)

Habitat: dry woodland clearings, barrens, ridges, and adjacent grassy landscapes

Broods: one generation; larvae likely overwinter; biennial

Abundance: rare to common; local

Range: northern Minnesota, Wisconsin, and Michigan

Compare: Chryxus Arctic (pg. 181) is less orange above, is more boldly patterned on the ventral hindwing, and lacks white veins

Comments: This large and distinctive arctic is primarily a Canadian species, but its range dips southward into the US only in northern Minnesota and the Upper Peninsula of Michigan. Macoun's Arctic is an understudied butterfly in our region, and many aspects of its biology and ecology remain poorly known. Adults have a fairly weak flight and regularly perch on tree branches or trunks where they can be easily overlooked. The larvae require two years to develop. Adults have synchronous flight in even-numbered years.

Macoun's Arctic

Oeneis macounii

Family/Subfamily: Brush-Footed Butterflies (Nymphalidae)/ Satyrs and Wood-Nymphs (Satyrinae)

Wingspan: 1.6–2.1" (4.1–5.3 cm)

Above: light orange brown with darker margins; forewing has two prominent black eyespots with white "pupils" (often with one or more adjacent smaller black spots); hindwing has a small black eyespot near anal angle

Below: hindwing is mottled brown and gray, with fine striations and a darker median band

Sexes: similar

Egg: cream, laid singly near host

Larva: green to light brown with green and darker brown strips

Larval Host Plants: unknown; likely various grasses or sedges

Habitat: dry woodland clearings, open pine forests, margins and trails, and adjacent open areas

Broods: one generation; larvae likely overwinter; biennial

Abundance: rare to uncommon; local

Range: northern Minnesota and Michigan

dorsal

Compare: Appalachian Brown (pg. 199) has a smoother, more sinuous ventral postmedian line on the hindwing; the middle two eyespots on the ventral forewing are generally smaller than those above or below

Comments: The Eyed Brown is a delicate butterfly of open, sedge-dominated wetland habitats. As a result, populations tend to be spotty and localized. Nonetheless, the butterfly can be quite abundant when encountered but seldom strays far from host resources. Adults have a slow, bouncing flight and traverse low through wetland vegetation, stopping to perch where they are easily overlooked. They periodically bask with their wings partially open.

Eyed Brown

Lethe eurydice

Family/Subfamily: Brush-Footed Butterflies (Nymphalidae)/ Satyrs and Wood-Nymphs (Satyrinae)

Wingspan: 1.6–2.25" (4.1–5.7 cm)

Above: light brown (occasionally darker) with a submarginal row of black eyespots; those on the hindwing have pale outlines

Below: light brown; forewing has straight, uniform row of four double-rimmed black eyespots; hindwing has a row of five to six double-rimmed black eyespots with pale centers, bordered inwardly by a dark, jagged postmedian line

Sexes: similar, although female generally paler brown and has larger eyespots

Egg: light yellow green, round, laid singly on or near host leaves

Larva: light green with narrow longitudinal yellow stripes, a dark-green dorsal stripe, two short tails, and two reddish horns off the head

Larval Host Plants: various sedges (*Carex* spp.)

Habitat: marshes, sedge meadows, fens, roadside ditches, and adjacent habitats

Broods: one generation; larvae overwinter

Abundance: occasional to common; local

Range: primarily northern half of the region

Compare: Chryxus Arctic (pg. 181) is more boldly patterned on the ventral hindwing and is found in dry habitats

Comments: This widespread boreal species extends southward into the US in the Rocky Mountains and northern portions of the Upper Midwest. It is restricted to forested bogs, where it is usually encountered near the protected confines of more wooded margins. It tends not to prefer more-open areas. Populations tend to be highly localized. Adults often perch on tree trunks and fly rapidly if disturbed. The Jutta Arctic requires two seasons to complete larval development.

Jutta Arctic
Oeneis jutta

Family/Subfamily: Brush-Footed Butterflies (Nymphalidae)/ Satyrs and Wood-Nymphs (Satyrinae)

Wingspan: 1.7–2.1" (4.3–5.3 cm)

Above: dull gray brown; forewing has yellow-brown submarginal band enclosing (typically) one to three small black eyespots; hindwing has yellow-brown submarginal band enclosing a single black eyespot at the anal angle

Below: forewing as above; hindwing is mottled brown and gray with fine striations and thin, dark, jagged median line bordered outwardly by gray

Sexes: similar

Egg: pale yellow, laid singly and haphazardly near host

Larva: light brown with darker brown and cream lateral strips

Larval Host Plants: various sedges, including cottongrass (*Eriophorum* spp.)

Habitat: open Black Spruce bogs and bog margins

Broods: one generation; larvae likely overwinter; biennial

Abundance: rare to occasional; local

Range: northern Minnesota, Wisconsin, and Michigan

Compare: unique; California Tortoiseshell is a rare vagrant to our region

Comments: This small but electric tortoiseshell has to be seen to be truly appreciated. The dorsal colors are in stark contrast to the highly cryptic, bark-like pattern of the wings below. Particularly common in the Upper Midwest, its population numbers tent to vary considerably from year to year and can at time be particularly abundant. Unlike many other anglewings, the adults frequently visit flowers in addition to fermenting fruit, tree sap, dung, and other food sources.

Milbert's Tortoiseshell
Aglais milberti

Family/Subfamily: Brush-Footed Butterflies (Nymphalidae)/ True Brush-Foots (Nymphalinae)

Wingspan: 1.75–2.4" (4.4–6.1 cm)

Above: chocolate brown with a broad, orange (fading to golden orange inwardly) submarginal band; forewing apex is extended and squared off with a white apical spot and two orange cell bars; hindwing has a marginal row of small blue spots and a short, stubby tail; wing margins are irregular

Below: strongly two-toned with striated, bark-like pattern; basal half is blackish brown and outer portion is lighter gray brown

Sexes: similar

Egg: small, green, barrel-shaped, laid clusters on host leaves

Larva: black with two pale lateral bands, white speckling, and several rows of black, branched spines; ventral surface is green; young larvae live in a communal silken nest, become solitary with age

Larval Host Plants: Stinging Nettle (*Urtica dioica*)

Habitat: wet meadows, stream margins, forest edges and openings, and adjacent open sites

Broods: two or more generations; adults overwinter; some pupae may overwinter

Abundance: uncommon to common; can be periodically abundant in our region

Range: primarily northern portions of the region; also extreme western portions

Compare: Hoary Edge (pg. 171) is smaller and has marginal dirty-white ventral hindwing patch; Golden-banded Skipper (pg. 176) lacks ventral white hindwing patch

Comments: The Silver-spotted Skipper is a large, robust-bodied butterfly named for the conspicuous clear white, irregular-shaped patch on the hindwing below that is easily seen with the naked eye. They are one of our most commonly encountered large skippers. Adults have a fast, powerful flight that offers a challenging pursuit. Fortunately, they are fond of flowers and regular pause to feed, making them a frequent garden visitor. The colorful larvae construct individual leaf shelters on the host by weaving leaves together with silk. They forcibly (and somewhat comically) jettison their frass (poop) from these shelters to help reduce detection from predators.

Silver-Spotted Skipper

Epargyreus clarus

Family/Subfamily: Skippers (Hesperiidae)/
Dicot Skippers (Eudaminae)

Wingspan: 1.75–2.4" (4.4–6.1 cm)

Above: brown; forewing is elongated with a median row of gold
spots; hindwing is tapered to a small, rounded, lobe-like tail;
wing fringes are checkered

Below: forewing as above with pinkish frosting along margin;
hindwing has a distinct, elongated clear white median patch

Sexes: similar

Egg: light green, laid singly on host leaves

Larva: yellow green with darker transverse lines; bulbous
reddish-brown head with two orange spots

Larval Host Plants: pea family (Fabaceae) plants, including Black
Locust (*Robinia pseudoacacia*), American Wisteria (*Wisteria
frutescens*), Chinese Wisteria (*Wisteria sinensis*), False Indigo
(*Amorpha fruticosa*), and Kudzu (*Pueraria montana*)

Habitat: open woodlands and margins, brush fields, roadsides,
old fields, parks, and gardens

Broods: two or more generations; pupae overwinter

Abundance: occasional to common

Range: throughout

ventral

Compare: Southern Pearly-Eye (not pictured) enters our region only in southern Missouri and has orange antennal clubs

Comments: This is a large, reclusive butterfly primarily of shaded woodlands and wetlands. While generally not uncommon, populations are often highly localized and found in close association with patches of larval hosts; can be locally common when encountered. Adults have a quick, somewhat bobbing flight and maneuver close to the ground. They frequently alight on low vegetation, tree trunks, or the ground. They do not visit flowers but instead feed on sap flows, rotting fruit, decaying vegetation, fungi, and animal dung. Unlike most butterflies, the Northern Pearly-Eye is active on overcast days and often flies well into the evening hours.

Northern Pearly-Eye

Lethe anthedon

Family/Subfamily: Brush-Footed Butterflies (Nymphalidae)/ Satyrs and Wood-Nymphs (Satyrinae)

Wingspan: 1.75–2.6" (4.3–6.6 cm)

Above: warm brown with pale-outlined, solid-black eyespots on a somewhat lighter brown field; hindwing has a slightly scalloped margin; antennal clubs are orange with a black base

Below: warm brown with a violet cast; forewing has a straight row of four yellow-rimmed black eyespots; hindwing has cream-outlined submarginal area enclosing a row of yellow-rimmed black eyespots with light highlights and two darker brown median lines

Sexes: similar, although female generally has broader, more rounded wings and larger eyespots

Egg: greenish white, round, laid singly on host leaves

Larva: yellow green with narrow longitudinal yellow stripes, a dark-green dorsal stripe, two short red-tipped tails, and two reddish horns off the head

Larval Host Plants: various grasses, including Whitegrass (*Leersia virginica*), Indian Woodoats (*Chasmanthium latifolium*), Bearded Shorthusk (*Brachyelytrum erectum*), plumegrass (*Dichelachne* spp.), and Reed Canarygrass (*Phalaris arundinacea*); may also use some sedges (*Carex* spp.)

Habitat: moist, shaded woodlands and margins, stream corridors, marsh edges, and fens

Broods: one generation; larvae overwinter

Abundance: uncommon to common; local

Range: throughout, except far western portions of the region

Compare: unique

Comments: A large, drab skipper of the Deep South, it strays northward, occasionally making its into way our region. It is unable to survive freezing temperatures in any life stage. Also called the Canna Leaf Roller, larvae make leaf shelters on cannas (*Canna* spp.) and can be a nuisance. Adults have narrow wings and a noticeably long proboscis. They have a strong, rapid flight and visit a range of flowers.

Brazilian Skipper
Calpodes ethlius

Family/Subfamily: Skippers (Hesperiidae)/
Grass-Skippers (Hesperiinae)

Wingspan: 1.8–2.2" (4.6–5.6 cm)

Above: dull dark brown; elongated forewing with prominent
glassy spots

Below: hindwing is brown to reddish brown with three to four
prominent glassy spots

Sexes: similar

Egg: gray-green, laid singly on host leaves

Larva: green with shiny transparent cuticle and an orange head
marked by black

Larval Host Plants: Alligator Flag (*Thalia geniculata*), Indian Shot
(*Canna indica*), and Garden Canna (*Canna x generalis*)

Habitat: wetlands, parks, and gardens

Broods: one or more generations; does not overwinter in
our region

Abundance: uncommon to rare

Range: extreme southern portions of the region;
strays northward

nephele

Compare: unique

Comments: This is one of our largest and most distinctive satyrs. Living up to its name, the species is also arguably the most commonly encountered. The Common Wood-Nymph occurs throughout most of the US and southern Canada. In our region, it is geographically variable. Populations with distinctive yellow forewing patches occur in the southern portions of the region, while those farther north are predominantly brown. Intermediate forms can also be found. Adults are opportunistic feeders, visiting flowers along with sap flows and rotting fruit.

Common Wood-Nymph

Cercyonis pegala

Family/Subfamily: Brush-Footed Butterflies (Nymphalidae)/
Satyrs and Wood-Nymphs (Satyrinae)

Wingspan: 1.8–2.8" (4.6–7.1 cm)

Above: brown; subspecies *alope* (southern portions) has two
white-centered black forewing eyespots inside a large yellow
patch; subspecies *nephele* lacks the yellow forewing patch

Below: brown with dark striations; subspecies *alope* (southern
portions) has two white-centered black forewing eyespots
inside a large yellow patch; subspecies *nephele* lacks
the yellow forewing patch; hindwings may have several
small eyespots

Sexes: similar, although females are paler and have
larger eyespots

Egg: yellow cream, laid singly on host leaves

Larva: green with a dark-green dorsal stripe, yellow lateral
stripe, and two short tails

Larval Host Plants: various grasses, including bluestem
(*Schizachyrium* spp.), Poverty Oatgrass (*Danthonia spicata*),
and Purpletop Tridens (*Tridens flava*)

Habitat: wet meadows, old fields, prairies, open woodlands and
margins, and wet meadows

Broods: one generation; larvae overwinter

Abundance: occasional to abundant

Range: throughout

Compare: Eyed Brown (pg. 185) has a noticeably more jagged ventral postmedian line on the hindwing; the ventral forewing has a submarginal row of four black eyespots of similar size

Comments: Although this butterfly is called the Appalachian Brown, its range extends from central Florida to southern Canada and west to Minnesota and Missouri. It tends to be confined more to wet woodlands and shaded swamps compared to open sedge meadows, as is the case with the similar-looking Eyed Brown. That said, close examination is required for accurate identification in the field. Like other wetland species, populations tend to be highly localized. Adults do not visit flowers but instead feed on sap flows, fermenting fruit and organic material, and animal dung.

Appalachian Brown

Lethe appalachia

Family/Subfamily: Brush-Footed Butterflies (Nymphalidae)/ Satyrs and Wood-Nymphs (Satyrinae)

Wingspan: 1.9–2.25" (4.8–5.7 cm)

Above: light brown with a submarginal row of black eyespots; eyespots on the hindwing have pale outlines

Below: light brown; forewing has a straight, uniform row of four double-rimmed black eyespots, the middle pair generally somewhat smaller than the one above or below; hindwing has a row of five to six double-rimmed black eyespots with pale centers, bordered inwardly by a dark, sinuous postmedian line

Sexes: similar, although female is generally paler brown and has larger eyespots

Egg: greenish white, round, laid singly on or near host leaves

Larva: light green with narrow longitudinal yellow stripes, a dark-green dorsal stripe, two short tails, and two reddish horns off the head

Larval Host Plants: various sedges (*Carex* spp.)

Habitat: wet woodlands, wooded swamps, moist grassy glades, forested stream corridors, bogs, and wetland margins

Broods: one generation; larvae overwinter

Abundance: occasional to common; local

Range: primarily the eastern two-thirds of the region

ventral

Compare: Tawny Emperor (pg. 203) is more orange brown above; dorsal forewing lacks the white apical spots and single post-median eyespot; the two species are often seen together

Comments: This mostly brown butterfly is named after its preferred larval host. A denizen of rich woods and other sites that support hackberry, it may also be encountered in urban parks, yards, and neighborhoods. Adults have a strong, rapid flight and often perch on sunlit leaves, overhanging branches, or tree trunks along forest trails and margins. They are exceedingly pugnacious and inquisitive, and they readily dart out to investigate most any passing object, occasionally even landing on humans. Although often localized in occurrence, the Hackberry Emperor can be quite abundant when encountered.

Hackberry Emperor
Asterocampa celtis

Family/Subfamily: Brush-Footed Butterflies (Nymphalidae)/ Emperors (Apaturinae)

Wingspan: 2.0–2.6" (5.1–6.6 cm)

Above: amber brown; forewing has a black apex enclosing numerous white spots and a single submarginal black eyespot; hindwing has an irregular black submarginal line and a postmedian row of black spots

Below: as above with muted coloration; hindwing has a postmedian row of yellow-rimmed black spots with blue-green centers

Sexes: similar, although female is larger and has noticeably broader wings

Egg: creamy white, laid singly or more often in small clusters on the underside of host leaves

Larva: light green with two narrow yellow dorsal stripes; mottled with small yellow spots; dark head bears two stubby, branched horns; rear end has a pair of short tails

Larval Host Plants: Common Hackberry (*Celtis occidentalis*), Sugarberry (*Celtis laevigata*), and Dwarf Hackberry (*Celtis tenuifolia*)

Habitat: rich, deciduous woodlands; stream corridors; swamps; forest margins; woodland clearings and adjacent open areas; wooded yards; and neighborhoods

Broods: two generations; larvae overwinter

Abundance: occasional to common; localized

Range: throughout the southern two-thirds of the region; occasional to absent farther north

ventral

Compare: Hackberry Emperor (pg. 201) is brown above; dorsal forewing is black with white apical spots and single postmedian eyespot; the two species are often seen together

Comments: The Tawny Emperor shares its affinity for rich woodland habitats with the more common and widespread Hackberry Emperor. The two species are often found together but tend to be localized and seldom found far from stands of their host trees. The distinctive larvae are gregarious and continue to feed together until becoming more solitary as they mature. Partially grown larvae overwinter in small groups in a hibernaculum formed by tying leaves together with silk. Tawny Emperors commence feeding again in the spring and complete development.

Tawny Emperor

Asterocampa clyton

Family/Subfamily: Brush-Footed Butterflies (Nymphalidae)/ Emperors (Apaturinae)

Wingspan: 2.0–2.75" (5.1–7.0 cm)

Above: orange brown with dark markings and borders; forewing has a postmedian row of pale yellow-orange spots and two black cell bars; hindwings have a postmedian row of round black spots

Below: as above with muted gray-brown cast coloration; hindwing has a postmedian row of yellow-rimmed black spots with blue-green centers

Sexes: similar, although female is larger and has noticeably broader wings

Egg: creamy white, laid in large pyramidal-shaped clusters on the underside of host leaves

Larva: light green with narrow, dark-green dorsal stripes and broad, yellow-and-cream stripes; mottled with small yellow spots; green head bears two stubby, branched horns; rear end has a pair of short tails

Larval Host Plants: Common Hackberry (*Celtis occidentalis*), Sugarberry (*Celtis laevigata*), and Dwarf Hackberry (*Celtis tenuifolia*)

Habitat: rich, deciduous woodlands; stream corridors; swamps; forest margins; woodland clearings and adjacent open areas; wooded yards; and neighborhoods

Broods: one to two generations; larvae overwinter

Abundance: uncommon to occasional; localized

Range: throughout the southeastern two-thirds of the region; occasional to absent farther north and west

Yucca Giant-Skipper
Megathymus yuccae

Family/Subfamily: Skippers (Hesperiidae)/
Grass-Skippers (Hesperiinae)

Wingspan: 2.0–2.9" (5.1–7.4 cm)

Habitat: grasslands and mixed prairie

Range: southwestern portions, only Nebraska and Kansas

Sexes: similar

Larva: light tan to cream with a dark-brown head; feed on yucca

Above: forewings are elongated; robust body; dark-brown wings;
forewing has outer yellow spot band and small white spots
near the apex; hindwing has broad yellow margin in male;
hindwing in female has second partial postmedian yellow
spot band; females' wings are much larger and rounder

Below: forewing as above; hindwing is dark blackish brown
with extensive violet-gray frosting on the outer portion
and a prominent white spot along the leading margin

Compare: unique

Comments: A large and robust skipper. Widespread throughout
the southern US. Adults fly in spring.

Strecker's Giant-Skipper
Megathymus streckeri leussleri

Family/Subfamily: Skippers (Hesperiidae)/
Grass-Skippers (Hesperiinae)

Wingspan: 2.25–3.1" (5.7–7.9 cm)

Habitat: grasslands, mixed prairie, rocky bluffs, and woodlands

Range: western portions of the region

Sexes: similar

Larva: light tan to cream with a dark-brown head; feed on yucca

Above: forewings are elongated; robust body; wings are dark
brown; forewing has outer spot band made up of large yellow
spots; spots closest to apex become white; spot band is
broader in females; hindwing has a broad yellow margin in
male; hindwing in female has second partial postmedian yellow spot band; females' wings are much larger and rounder

Below: forewing as above; hindwing dark brown with gray
scaling and scattered white to creamy yellow spots

Compare: unique

Comments: Our largest skipper, it is widespread throughout the
High Plains. Strong fliers, they make audible sounds in the air.

ventral

Compare: Gray Comma (pg. 283) is smaller and lacks the broad black spots and white apical spots on the wings above

Comments: This is a large, somewhat distinctive boreal species of northern forests. Population numbers often fluctuate considerably from year to year, and it can have periodic outbreak years, during which it may wander farther south. Nonetheless, Gray Commas are most reliably encountered in more-northern areas. Adults have a quick, darting flight and are wary of close approach. They readily bask with their wings open in sunlit patches on gravel roads, logs, or tree trunks. Adults do not visit flowers but are particularly fond of fermenting fruit and tree sap.

Compton Tortoiseshell
Nymphalis vaualbum

Family/Subfamily: Brush-Footed Butterflies (Nymphalidae)/ True Brush-Foots (Nymphalinae)

Wingspan: 2.5–3.1" (6.4–7.9 cm)

Above: orange brown with heavy black spots and golden scaling toward the outer margin; each wing bears a white spot near the apex; forewing apex is extended and squared off; hindwing has a short, stubby tail; irregular wing margins

Below: heavily mottled and bark-like pattern; somewhat two-toned; darker brown basally, noticeably paler brown on outer half

Sexes: similar

Egg: small, green, laid in clusters on host

Larva: somewhat variable; light green with cream spots, longitudinal reddish or blackish stripes, and lateral cream and dorsal black branched spines

Larval Host Plants: various trees, including birch (*Betula* spp.), elm (*Ulmus* spp.), and Quaking Aspen (*Populus tremuloides*)

Habitat: deciduous or mixed forests and associated clearings, trails, and margins; wooded yards

Broods: one generation; adults overwinter

Abundance: uncommon to occasional

Range: primarily throughout the northeastern portion of the region

ventral

Compare: cannot easily be confused with any other butterfly

Comments: Appropriately named, the Giant Swallowtail is the largest butterfly in the Midwest. Despite its fairly widespread distribution, it is seldom overly common, especially in northern areas, with populations often being quite local. When seen however, the sizable adults are distinctive. They are quite fond of flowers and continuously flutter their wings while feeding. Adults have a strong, somewhat gliding flight. The distinctively mottled larvae resemble bird droppings. If disturbed, they extend a bright-red osmeterium from behind the head. This fleshy defensive organ emits a foul odor and chemical irritant that helps repel many predators and parasitoids.

Giant Swallowtail

Papilio cresphontes

Family/Subfamily: Swallowtails (Papilionidae)/
Swallowtails (Papilioninae)

Wingspan: 4.5–5.5" (11.4–14 cm)

Above: chocolate brown with broad, crossing yellow spot bands
that form an "X" on the forewing; one of the spot bands
extends from the tip of the forewing to the base of the abdomen; orange-and-black eyespot near single, yellow-centered
hindwing tail

Below: creamy yellow with brown markings; hindwing has a
central dark band marked with blue and orange

Sexes: similar, although females are generally larger

Egg: amber brown, round, laid singly on host leaves

Larva: brown with yellow and cream patches; resembles a bird
dropping; extends orange osmeterium when disturbed

Larval Host Plants: various citrus family (Rutaceae) plants,
including Common Prickly Ash (*Zanthoxylum americanum*)
and Common Hoptree (*Ptelea trifoliata*),

Habitat: deciduous forests and nearby open areas, including
pastures, wetlands, roadsides, meadows, and rural gardens

Broods: two generations; pupae overwinter

Abundance: uncommon to occasional; more common southward

Range: primarily southern two-thirds of region; absent from
northern Michigan, Wisconsin, and North Dakota; rare in
South Dakota, uncommon in much of Nevada and Kansas

Compare: unique

Comments: This small skipper is quickly recognized by its black-and-white checkerboard pattern. Widespread and generally common across much of the central and southern US, it expands its range to temporarily colonize many northern locations each year. As a result, the Common Checkered-Skipper may often be more frequently encounter in late summer or fall in most parts of our region. The species is unable to survive harsh winter temperatures in any life stage. The small adults scurry over weedy vegetation with a quick, erratic fight. The larvae construct individual leaf shelters on the host. When mature, they pupate inside the shelters.

Common Checkered-Skipper

Burnsius communis

Family/Subfamily: Skippers (Hesperiidae)/
Spread-Wing Skippers (Pyrginae)

Wingspan: 0.75–1.25" (1.9–3.2 cm)

Above: dark gray brown with scattered white spots; male has
extensive blue-gray hairs on wing bases and body; female
lacks hairs and thus appears much darker

Below: white with tan to brown irregular bands and spots

Sexes: similar, although female lacks blue-gray hairs and
appears much darker

Egg: yellow green, laid singly on host leaves

Larva: pale gray green with dark-green dorsal stripe, pale lateral
stripes and a black head; body covered in small white dots

Larval Host Plants: various mallow family (Malvaceae) plants,
including Common Mallow (*Malva neglecta*), globemallow
(*Sphaeralcea* spp.), and Hollyhock (*Alcea rosea*)

Habitat: open, disturbed sites, including roadsides, weedy fields,
fallow agricultural lands, utility easements, and gardens

Broods: one or more generations; pupae overwinter

Abundance: rare to common

Range: throughout, although most common in southern portions; rare to uncommon in northern portions

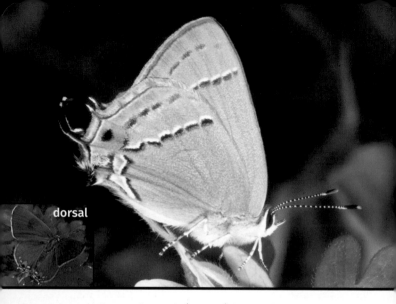

dorsal

Compare: Acadian Hairstreak (pg. 217) has white-outlined black spots and a conspicuous submarginal row of orange spots on the ventral hindwings; restricted to wetlands with willows

Comments: This is one of the most common, frequently encountered hairstreaks in the Midwest. Adults have an affinity for most open, sunny, and often-disturbed sites where their often somewhat weedy hosts occur. The Gray Hairstreak is also regular garden visitor, being quite fond of flowers. Adults often perch on vegetation with their wings partially open, an unusual behavior for most hairstreaks. The small hair-like tails near the prominent hindwing eyespot resemble a "false head" and help deflect a predator's attack away from the insect's vulnerable body. This charade, employed by many members of the family, is enhanced by a regular up-and-down motion of the hindwings once landed.

Gray Hairstreak
Strymon melinus

Family/Subfamily: Gossamer Wings (Lycaenidae)/ Hairstreaks (Theclinae)

Wingspan: 1.0–1.3" (2.5–3.8 cm)

Above: slate gray with an orange-capped black spot near hindwing tail

Below: light gray with a black-and-white line across both wings (often with some orange); hindwing has an orange-capped black spot and blue scaling near hindwing tail

Sexes: similar

Egg: light green, flattened, disc-shaped, laid singly on host flower buds or flowers

Larva: slug-like, variable, bright green with cream lateral stripe to pinkish red

Larval Host Plants: wide variety of plants, including clover (*Trifolium* spp.), milkpea (*Galactia* spp.), Common Partridge Pea (*Chamaecrista fasciculata*), various beans (*Phaseolus* spp.), lespedeza (*Lespedeza* spp.), vetch (*Vicia* spp.), and mallow (*Malva* spp.).

Habitat: open, disturbed sites, including roadsides, easements, fallow agricultural land, old fields, pastures, and gardens; also woodland margins, prairies, and rural meadows.

Broods: two or more generations; eggs overwinter

Abundance: occasional to common

Range: throughout

Compare: Bronze Copper (pg. 249) is somewhat smaller but has purplish-brown to orange dorsal forewings

Comments: This often-reclusive species is our largest copper. Aptly named, the adults are dark gray above and light gray below. A butterfly of primarily moist habitats, the Gray Copper tends to be highly localized but can often be common when encountered. Adults are fond of flowers and are often spotted when feeding. Females lay eggs at the base of host plants on living or dead leaves and stems. The eggs overwinter, and larvae complete development the following spring.

Gray Copper
Lycaena dione

Family/Subfamily: Gossamer Wings (Lycaenidae)/ Coppers (Lycaeninae)

Wingspan: 1.25–1.7" (3.2–4.3 cm)

Above: dark brown-gray wings; female has black forewing spots and a scalloped orange submarginal band on hindwing subtended by black spots; males may have no or reduced orange submarginal band

Below: white gray with scattered black spots; hindwing has a partial wavy orange submarginal band subtended by black spots

Sexes: dissimilar; female has black dorsal forewing spots and prominent orange submarginal band on dorsal hindwing

Egg: whitish, turban-shaped, laid singly on host stems or leaves

Larva: slug-like, yellow green to green

Larval Host Plants: native and nonnative dock (*Rumex* spp.)

Habitat: open, primarily moist sites, including wet meadows, marshes, wet fields and ditches, and adjacent open areas

Broods: one generation; eggs overwinter

Abundance: rare to locally common; declining and of conservation concern in Wisconsin

Range: western portion of the region; absent east of Wisconsin and Illinois

Compare: Coral Hairstreak (pg. 125) is browner and lacks hind-wing tail; Edwards' Hairstreak (pg. 117) has gray-brown ventral hindwings and is typically found in drier habitats with oaks; Gray Copper (pg. 215) is larger and lacks hindwing tail

Comments: This showy hairstreak is restricted to wetland habitats or other moist sites that support its willow hosts. Although fairly widespread, the species tends to occur in smaller, highly localized colonies but can often be fairly common when encountered. The adults have a quick flight but readily visit at moisture-loving flowers. Acadian Hairstreaks are particularly fond of milkweed blooms.

Acadian Hairstreak
Satyrium acadica

Family/Subfamily: Gossamer Wings (Lycaenidae)/ Hairstreaks (Theclinae)

Wingspan: 1.1–1.45" (2.8–3.6 cm)

Above: brown with small orange crescent-shaped spot above hindwing tail

Below: uniform light gray with postmedian row of round, white-rimmed black spots; hindwing has a submarginal row of orange spots and an orange-capped blue spot near the tail

Sexes: similar

Egg: whitish, flattened, disc-shaped, laid singly on host twigs

Larva: slug-like, green with pale oblique dorsal dashes and white lateral stripe

Larval Host Plants: various willows (*Salix* spp.)

Habitat: stream margins, pond edges, marshes, swamps, wet roadside ditches, bogs, and moist meadows

Broods: single generation; pupae overwinter

Abundance: occasional to common; localized

Range: northern and central portions of the region

Red-Banded Hairstreak

Calycopus cecrops

Family/Subfamily: Gossamer Wings (Lycaenidae)/ Hairstreaks (Theclinae)

Wingspan: 0.75–1.0" (1.9–2.5 cm)

Habitat: woodlands, forest margins, brushy areas, wooded yards

Range: southernmost portions of the region

Sexes: similar; female has more blue scaling on wings above

Larva: slug-like, pinkish brown and covered in short hairs

Above: male is slate gray with no markings; female is slate gray with iridescent blue scaling on hindwing; hindwing has two short, white-tipped tails

Below: light gray with broad, red postmedian band edged outwardly in white and black; hindwing with blue scaling and dark eyespots near the tails

Compare: unique

Comments: Red-Banded Hairstreak females do not lay eggs directly on their host plants. Instead, they land on the ground beneath their hosts and deposit eggs singly on the underside of dead leaves and other fallen debris.

Early Hairstreak
Erora laeta

Family/Subfamily: Gossamer Wings (Lycaenidae)/
Hairstreaks (Theclinae)

Wingspan: 0.75–1.0" (9–2.5 cm)

Habitat: beech forests and associated margins, roadsides, trails,
clearings, and stream corridors

Range: extreme southeast portion of the range (southern Ohio);
rare strays in Michigan and Wisconsin

Sexes: similar, although female has more blue dorsal scaling

Larva: slug-like, yellow green to greenish brown, reddish-
brown patches

Above: slate gray with blue scaling toward wing bases; tailless

Below: pale greenish gray with a band of white-rimmed,
reddish-orange spots across the wings; hindwing has a
row of smaller, white-rimmed, reddish-orange spots along
the outer margin

Compare: unique

Comments: This hairstreak spends much of its time in trees,
coming down only for nectar and puddles.

Compare: unique

Comments: Strikingly colored, this is arguably one of our most attractive hairstreaks. The Juniper Hairstreak typically occurs in spotty, highly localized colonies but can be somewhat common when encountered. As its name suggests, adults are always found in close association with stands of Eastern Redcedar, its sole larval host. The relationship is so intimate that adult butterflies spend much of their lives within the canopy of host trees, venturing down only occasionally to nectar or possibly disperse to pioneer new colony sites. Because of this behavior, the small adults can often go unnoticed. They are often best encountered by gently tapping the trunk or branches with a net handle or long pole.

Juniper Hairstreak
Callophrys gryneus

Family/Subfamily: Gossamer Wings (Lycaenidae)/ Hairstreaks (Theclinae)

Wingspan: 0.8–1.1" (2.0–2.8 cm)

Above: variable; unmarked brown to brown with extensive amber scaling; hindwing with two short tails; male has pale gray forewing stigma

Below: variable; bright olive green; forewing has straight submarginal white band and reddish-brown scaling along trailing edge; hindwing has two white bars toward the base and an irregular white postmedian band that is edged on the inside with reddish brown

Sexes: similar, although male has pale ventral forewing stigma

Egg: light green, turban-shaped, laid singly on host

Larva: slug-like, green with bold white lines and dashes

Larval Host Plants: Eastern Redcedar (*Juniperus virginiana*)

Habitat: sites with redcedar, including forest edges, barrens, windbreaks, rocky outcrops, dry hillsides, roadsides, old fields, and cemeteries

Broods: two generations; pupae overwinter

Abundance: uncommon to occasional; localized

Range: southern two-thirds of the region

Compare: European Skipper (pg. 227) has less rounded wings, is somewhat more grayish orange below, and has narrow black dorsal wing borders; also is not restricted to wet habitats

Comments: The Least Skipper is a small, easy-to-identify butterfly of primarily wet habitats. Highly adaptable to human disturbance, it may be encountered in high-quality wetlands to moist roadside drainage ditches, provided that suitable host resources are available. Widespread but often somewhat local in occurrence, it can at times be exceedingly abundant under the right circumstances. Adults have a weak flight and flutter slowly through grasses and other vegetation, landing frequently on sunlit leaves or available flowers. The slender larvae construct individual tube-like shelters on the host by rolling grass blades over and securing them lengthwise with silk.

Least Skipper

Ancyloxypha numitor

Family/Subfamily: Skippers (Hesperiidae)/
Grass-Skippers (Hesperiinae)

Wingspan: 0.7–1.0" (1.8–2.5 cm)

Above: wings are rounded and orange with broad black borders;
forewing has variable amounts of dark scaling and can occasionally appear almost entirely black

Below: forewing is black with a broad orange border; hindwing
is all orange with slightly lighter veins

Sexes: similar, although male has a longer, pointed abdomen
that extends beyond the wings

Egg: yellow, laid singly on host leaves

Larva: elongate and slender; pale green with a darker green
dorsal stripe; head is reddish brown with cream stripes

Larval Host Plants: various grasses, including Rice Cutgrass
(*Leersia oryzoides*), Giant Cutgrass (*Zizaniopsis miliacea*),
panicgrass (*Panicum* spp.), and cordgrass (*Spartina* spp.)

Habitat: moist, grassy areas, including wet meadows, wetland
margins, and roadside ditches

Broods: two or more generations; larvae overwinter

Abundance: occasional to abundant

Range: throughout, although less common in extreme western
portions of the region

Arctic Skipper
Carterocephalus palaemon

Family/Subfamily: Skippers (Hesperiidae)/
Skipperlings (Heteropterinae)

Wingspan: 0.8–1.25" (2.0–3.2 cm)

Habitat: open woodlands, trails, moist meadows

Range: northeast portions of the region; uncommon to common

Sexes: similar

Larva: whitish green with a darker green dorsal stripe, cream or yellow lateral stripes, and a green head

Above: dark brown with numerous light orange spots

Below: forewing is yellow orange with dark-brown spots; hind-wing is yellow orange with dark brown-rimmed cream to white spots

Compare: unique

Comments: This small species is one of our most distinctive skippers. Widespread across boreal North America, its range extends into portions of the Upper Midwest and New England. Adults have a low, weak flight and perch with their wings open.

Swamp Metalmark
Calephelis muticum

Family/Subfamily: Metalmarks (Riodinidae)/
Metalmarks (Riodininae)

Wingspan: 1.0–1.2" (2.5–3.0 cm)

Habitat: wet meadows and alkaline fens

Range: restricted to Wisconsin, Indiana, and Missouri;
rare; localized

Sexes: similar, although female has broader, rounder wings

Larva: green with tiny black spots; covered in long whitish hairs

Above: reddish brown with numerous dark markings and two
narrow, metallic grayish-blue bands through the outer half

Below: marked similarly to dorsal surface but brighter orange

Compare: Northern Metalmark (pg. 92)

Comments: Populations are of conservation concern or listed as
endangered in several states. Adults scurry low to the ground
and frequently stop to perch with their wings outstretched.
During inclement weather or if disturbed, they often fly
quickly and land out of sight on the underside of leaves.

ventral

Compare: Least Skipper (pg. 223) has more-rounded wings, has broad black dorsal wing borders, and is more associated with wet habitats

Comments: This diminutive species was accidentally introduced into Ontario, Canada, from Europe in 1910, where it is known as the Essex Skipper. It continues to expand its range, capitalizing on the broad availability and transport of several nonnative grasses that are primarily used for livestock grazing, silage, and hay. The European Skipper is highly adaptable to urban settings, where it is a frequent sight in gardens, yards, and vacant lots. Adults maneuver low to the ground among grassy vegetation with slow and somewhat erratic flight, and they are very fond of available flowers.

European Skipper

Thymelicus lineola

Family/Subfamily: Skippers (Hesperiidae)/
Grass-Skippers (Hesperiinae)

Wingspan: 0.9–1.1" (2.3–2.8 cm)

Above: bronzy orange with narrow black borders; veins are darkened toward the outer wing margins; forewing in male has a narrow black stigma; short antennae

Below: hindwing is unmarked orange, often appearing a bit grayish orange

Sexes: similar, although male is brighter above with a narrow black forewing stigma

Egg: white, laid in rows on host

Larva: pale green with a darker green dorsal stripe and cream-yellow lateral stripes; head is greenish tan marked with two cream stripes

Larval Host Plants: various nonnative grasses, including Timothy (*Phleum pratense*), orchardgrass (*Dactylis* spp.), and Common Velvetgrass (*Holcus lanatus*)

Habitat: open grassy areas, meadows, old fields, roadsides, pastures, parks, and gardens

Broods: one generation; eggs overwinter

Abundance: occasional to abundant

Range: primarily the Great Lakes states

dorsal

Compare: Bronze Copper (pg. 249) is larger and has a light-gray ventral hindwing with a broad orange submarginal band

Comments: Although this butterfly species is called the American Copper, many authorities suggest that eastern US population may have resulted from historical, unintentional introductions from Europe. This argument is fueled by the species' preference for open, disturbed habitats and because it uses weedy, nonnative host plants as a larval host. Populations tend to be widespread and often localized but can be abundant when encountered. Adults frequently perch on bare ground or on low vegetation with wings partially open, revealing their lustrous coppery-colored forewings.

American Copper

Lycaena phlaeas

Family/Subfamily: Gossamer Wings (Lycaenidae)/
Coppers (Lycaeninae)

Wingspan: 0.9–1.3" (2.3–3.6 cm.)

Above: orange with brown-to-black spots, patches, and borders

Below: bright red-orange forewings with black spots and dark
borders; hindwing is gray with a wide, scalloped submarginal
orange band bordered by black spots

Sexes: similar, although female has more rounded wings

Egg: greenish white, turban-shaped, laid singly on host stems
or leaves

Larva: slug-like, variable color; yellow green to rose, often with a
narrow lateral stripe

Larval Host Plants: sheep sorrel (*Rumex acetosella*) and curly
dock (*Rumex crispus*)

Habitat: open, sunny, often-disturbed sites, including old fields,
pastures, roadsides, easements, and meadows

Broods: typically one to two generations; pupae overwinter

Abundance: occasional to abundnant

Range: throughout most of the region, and west to Nebraska
and the Dakotas

ventral

Compare: Dorcas Copper (pg. 85) is generally smaller and lacks or has a less extensive orange submarginal band on dorsal hindwing; female has less extensive orange dorsal scaling. Bog Copper (pg. 72) is smaller and restricted to acid bogs; not found in western portions of the region

Comments: Living up to its name, the Purplish Copper displays an iridescent purple sheen on the wings above. It is particularly stunning on fresh individuals when seen in bright sunlight. Fond of a variety of open, moist areas, populations tend to be small and somewhat localized but can be relatively abundant when encountered. While not as habitat restricted as many other coppers, expanding agricultural and urban development nonetheless continue to restrict the number of suitable wetland habitats available.

Purplish Copper

Lycaena helloides

Family/Subfamily: Gossamer Wings (Lycaenidae)/ Coppers (Lycaeninae)

Wingspan: 1.0–1.2" (2.5–3.0 cm)

Above: male is brown with strong purplish iridescence and scattered black spots, hindwings have a zigzag orange line along the lower margin; female is primarily orange with scattered black spots and broad brown borders

Below: forewing is orange with scattered black spots and purplish apex and outer margin; hindwing is purplish gray with small black spots and zigzag orange band along the outer margin

Sexes: dissimilar; female has increased orange scaling on the wings above

Egg: greenish white, turban-shaped, laid singly on host

Larva: slug-like, green with light-yellow stripes

Larval Host Plants: various knotweeds (*Polygonum* spp.) and docks (*Rumex* spp.)

Habitat: open, moist sites, including wet meadows, stream margins, roadside ditches, pond margins, marshes, and old fields

Broods: two to three generations; egg overwinter

Abundance: occasional to common; localized

Range: northern and western portions of the region

male

female

Compare: Sachem (pg. 133) lacks the small, scattered black spots on the ventral hindwing

Comments: The Fiery Skipper is abundant in many open, disturbed locations across the Deep South. A prolific colonizer, it readily expands its range northward each spring into portions of the Midwest, the Mid-Atlantic, Northeast, and even southern Ontario in Canada. This temporary range expansion is only expected to accelerate with climate warming. The butterfly is, however, unable to survive harsh winter temperatures. The larvae utilize a variety of lawn grasses and can become minor turf pests in some locations. Like many other skipper larvae, they construct individual leaf shelters on their host.

Fiery Skipper
Hylephila phyleus

Family/Subfamily: Skippers (Hesperiidae)/
Grass-Skippers (Hesperiinae)

Wingspan: 1.0–1.25" (2.5–3.2 cm)

Above: elongated wings; male is golden orange with a jagged black border and black forewing stigma; female is brown with orange spots and scaling along the leading margin of the forewing

Below: hindwing is bright orange in males or duller orange brown in females, with small, scattered black spots

Sexes: dissimilar; female is brown above and duller below, with larger black ventral hindwing spots

Egg: white, laid singly on host leaves

Larva: generally brown with darker stripes and a dark-brown head

Larval Host Plants: various grasses, including Kentucky Bluegrass (*Poa pratensis*), Bermudagrass (*Cynodon dactylon*), crabgrass (*Digitaria* spp.), and bentgrass (*Agrostis* spp.)

Habitat: open, grassy areas, including old fields, roadsides, vacant lots, meadows, forest margins and openings, parks, yards, and gardens

Broods: multiple generations where resident; broods do not overwinter in our region

Abundance: rare to occasional

Range: primarily southern portions of the region

Arogos Skipper
Atrytone arogos iowa

Family/Subfamily: Skippers (Hesperiidae)/
Grass-Skippers (Hesperiinae)

Wingspan: 1.0–1.5" (2.5–3.8 cm)

Habitat: prairie

Range: western portions of the region; rare; localized

Sexes: similar, although female is darker above with less extensive golden-orange scaling

Larva: green with a darker green dorsal stripe and a tan head marked with reddish stripes

Above: golden orange with dark-brown wing borders; female is darker with reduced orange; male lacks black stigma

Below: hindwing is an yellow orange with lighter veins

Compare: Delaware Skipper (pg. 237)

Comments: Restricted to high-quality prairie habitat, populations are small, highly fragmented, and critically imperiled throughout. Likely very sensitive to climate change and habitat management. Larvae feed on Little Bluestem (*Schizachyrium scoparium*) and Big Bluestem (*Andropogon gerardi*).

Arctic Fritillary

Boloria chariclea

Family/Subfamily: Brush-Footed Butterflies (Nymphalidae)/ Fritillaries and Longwings (Heliconiinae)

Wingspan: 1.2–1.5" (3.0–3.8 cm)

Habitat: bogs and adjacent forest margins

Range: extreme northern counties of Minnesota and northwest Wisconsin; rare to uncommon; very localized

Sexes: similar

Larva: blackish brown with light spots and short, black spines

Above: orange to light orange with black bands and spots

Below: reddish-brown hindwing with a complex pattern, including cream spots and lines; wing margins have thin cream spots; hindwing has a purplish cast

Compare: Freija Fritillary (pg. 250)

Comments: The subspecies *grandis* occurs in our region. It is restricted to bogs and their margins. Because of its similarity to other species, the remote nature of its distribution, and its often-far-flung habitat, additional understudied populations may occur. Also called the Purplish Fritillary.

Compare: Arogos Skipper (pg. 234) is very rare, inhabits only high-quality prairie habitat, and the male has a clear golden-orange forewing without the black cell-end bar; Byssus Skipper (pg. 261) is very similar above but has lighter forewing veins; hindwing is less uniform in color, with noticeably darker margins

Comments: The Delaware Skipper is a widespread and generally common skipper throughout much the eastern US. Highly adaptable, it can be found in a variety of moist or dry habitats from wetlands to barrens as well as yards and gardens. Despite this, it is seldom overly abundant. The golden-orange adults have a rapid, darting flight and readily perch on low sunlit vegetation. They also frequent available flowers. The larvae construct individual shelters of rolled or silk-tied grass leaves on the host.

Delaware Skipper

Anatrytone logan

Family/Subfamily: Skippers (Hesperiidae)/
Grass-Skippers (Hesperiinae)

Wingspan: 1.1–1.3" (2.8–3.3 cm)

Above: orange with dark-brown borders and veins; forewings
are elongated and somewhat pointed; male has a small
black cell-end bar but no stigma; female has dark-brown
scaling in forewing cell, wider borders, and larger forewing
cell-end bar

Below: unmarked golden orange

Sexes: similar, although female is darker dorsally with
reduced orange

Egg: white, laid singly on host

Larva: bluish white with fine dark spots, a black-and-white anal
plate, and a white head marked in black

Larval Host Plants: various grasses, including bluestem
(*Andropogon* spp.), plumegrass (*Dichelachne* spp.), and
Switchgrass (*Panicum virgatum*)

Habitat: open woodlands, forest margins, prairies, pastures,
meadows, wetland edges, old fields, and utility easements

Broods: one generation; larvae overwinter

Abundance: occasional to common

Range: throughout

Compare: unique

Comments: Distinctive in both appearance and behavior, the Harvester is the only North American butterfly with carnivorous larvae. The cryptic, slug-like larvae feed primarily on woolly aphids and even occasionally wear the aphid molts and carcasses for protection from predators. A denizen of woodland habitats, it is often found in highly localized colonies, in close association with populations of its host aphids. Adults feed on sugary aphid honeydew and seldom visit flowers. They are most often encountered while perched on sunlit vegetation.

Harvester
Feniseca tarquinius

Family/Subfamily: Gossamer Wings (Lycaenidae)/
Harvesters (Miletinae)

Wingspan: 1.1–1.3" (2.8–3.3 cm)

Above: orange with brown to black spots, patches, and borders

Below: orange brown to reddish brown; forewing has orange
central scaling and several dark patches outlined in white;
hindwing has numerous dark patches outlined in white and
frosted scaling toward base

Sexes: similar

Egg: greenish white, turban-shaped, laid singly among
aphid colonies

Larva: gray with whitish-yellow bumps, bordered with gray
brown along top; reddish-brown lateral stripes; and numerous short gray hairs

Larval Host Plants: does not feed on plant material; carnivorous
on woolly aphids

Habitat: forest margins, stream corridors, swamp edges, moist
woodlands and associated clearings, trails, and roads

Broods: typically one to two generations; pupae overwinter

Abundance: occasional; often highly localized

Range: throughout region but rare or absent from Dakotas

Compare: Silvery Checkerspot (pg. 259) has a postmedian row with some white-centered black spots above; ventral hind-wing lacks median row of arrowhead-shaped white spots

Comments: Although similar-looking dorsally to other checker-spots and crescents, the ornately patterned hindwing quickly differentiates the Gorgone Checkerspot from all others. These characteristic markings are most visible when adults are feeding at flowers. Populations tend to be widespread but somewhat localized throughout much of the central US. It is rare or absent on eastern portion of our range. Larvae are gregarious and feed together when young before becoming more solitary with age. Partially grown larvae overwinter.

Gorgone Checkerspot

Chlosyne gorgone

Family/Subfamily: Brush-Footed Butterflies (Nymphalidae)/ True Brush-Foots (Nymphalinae)

Wingspan: 1.1–1.5" (2.8–3.8 cm)

Above: tawny orange with black bands and spots; wing bases are heavily banded with black; hindwing has postmedian row of solid black spots and a full to partial row of pale crescent-shaped spots

Below: hindwing has a complex zigzag pattern, including a medial row of arrowhead-shaped white spots

Sexes: similar

Egg: small, pale green, laid in clusters on the underside of host leaves

Larva: yellow orange with black longitudinal stripes and several rows of short, branched black spines

Larval Host Plants: various aster family (Asteraceae) plants, including Great Ragweed (*Ambrosia trifida*), sunflower (*Helianthus* spp.), and coneflower (*Rudbeckia* spp.),

Habitat: open woodlands; prairie; stream corridors and adjacent dry, open grassy areas; old fields; and previously burned areas

Broods: one to two generations; larvae overwinter

Abundance: uncommon to occasional; local

Range: throughout central and western portions of the region

Compare: Leonard's Skipper (pg. 263) has a reddish-brown ventral hindwing with a paler spot band and flies in late summer

Comments: This early-season skipper is widespread throughout the Great Lakes and Northeast. In our region, it can be found from Minnesota southeast to Indiana and Ohio. Populations tend to be somewhat spotty and are generally more common northward. A highly active butterfly, the adult has a very rapid flight and nervously pauses to nectar at available flowers before darting off again.

Indian Skipper

Hesperia sassacus

Family/Subfamily: Skippers (Hesperiidae)/ Grass-Skippers (Hesperiinae)

Wingspan: 1.2–1.4" (3.0–3.6 cm)

Above: male is orange with wide, somewhat jagged dark-brown wing borders and a black forewing stigma; female has paler orange scaling

Below: hindwing is tawny orange to yellow orange with a lighter yellow spot band; the middle spot is displaced outward toward the margin

Sexes: similar, although female has somewhat broader dark borders and lighter yellow-orange markings, and it lacks the black forewing stigma

Egg: light green, laid singly on host leaves or stems

Larva: dark greenish brown, often with lighter mottling and a black head

Larval Host Plants: various grasses, including bluegrass (*Poa* spp.), panicgrass (*Panicum* spp.), Little Bluestem (*Schizachyrium scoparium*), and Red Fescue (*Festuca rubra*)

Habitat: woodland clearings and margins, pastures, old fields, roadsides, meadows, and utility easements

Broods: one generation; larvae overwinter

Abundance: uncommon to common; local

Range: northeastern portions of the region

Compare: Hobomok Skipper (pg. 165) male has more pronounced gray frosting along the ventral hindwing margin; ranges barely overlap

Comments: Distributed across portions of the Mountain West from southern Arizona and New Mexico north into Wyoming, the Taxiles Skipper's range range just extends into the westernmost portions of the Dakotas and Nebraska. The adults have one midsummer flight period annually and typically inhabit pine forest slopes and stream margins. Populations tend to be quite scattered and highly localized. Like many other species, the males perch in sunny locations for passing females and actively defend their territories.

Taxiles Skipper

Poanes taxiles

Family/Subfamily: Skippers (Hesperiidae)/
Grass-Skippers (Hesperiinae)

Wingspan: 1.2–1.6" (3.0–4.1 cm)

Above: male is orange with irregular, broad, dark-brown
wing borders; female is dark brown with more diffuse
orange markings

Below: hindwing in male is brown with a broad, irregular yellow
spot band in the center and a yellow basal spot; the centermost spot extends well past others toward the outer margin;
hindwing of female is purplish brown with purple-gray frosting along outer margin and in the lower center

Sexes: dissimilar; dorsal forewing is brown in females, with pale
dorsal forewing spots and no black stigma

Egg: round, cream-colored eggs laid singly on host leaves

Larva: light brown to tan with a red-brown head and white collar

Larval Host Plants: wheatgrass (*Agropyron* spp.), orchardgrass
(*Dactylis* spp.), and bentgrass (*Agrostis* spp.)

Habitat: forest margins and openings, stream margins

Broods: one generation; larvae overwinter

Abundance: rare to uncommon; localized

Range: extreme western portion of the region

ventral

Compare: Northern Crescent (pg. 265) is very similar above, but the hindwing has a larger, more open orange area; ventral hindwing has a large, dark marginal patch without a pale crescent in males

Comments: This is our most widespread and abundant crescent. The species is seemingly at home in virtually any open landscape with nearby larval hosts. The adults have a low, fluttering flight and are exceedingly fond of flowers, often showing a preference for composites. The Pearl Crescent gets its name from the small but obvious pale, crescent-shaped spot along the ventral margin of the hindwing. Young larvae are gregarious, becoming more solitary in later instars.

Pearl Crescent

Phyciodes tharos

Family/Subfamily: Brush-Footed Butterflies (Nymphalidae)/ True Brush-Foots (Nymphalinae)

Wingspan: 1.25–1.6" (3.2–4.1 cm)

Above: orange to tawny orange with black bands, spots, and wing borders; often appearing very dark; female is often somewhat paler, with a more golden-orange postmedian forewing band

Below: seasonally variable; hindwing is light brownish orange with dark marginal patch enclosing a pale crescent-shaped spot; cooler-season forms have a darker hindwing with increased pattern elements

Sexes: similar, although female is somewhat larger with somewhat-increased black markings and a paler postmedian forewing band

Egg: small, green, laid in clusters on the underside of host plant's leaves

Larva: dark brown to charcoal with lateral cream stripes and several rows of short, branched spines

Larval Host Plants: various asters (*Symphyotrichum* spp.)

Habitat: open, sunny habitats, including old fields, meadows, prairies, roadsides, forest margins and clearings, pastures, yards, and gardens

Broods: two or more generations; larvae overwinter

Abundance: occasional to abundant

Range: throughout

Compare: American Copper (pg. 229) and Purplish Copper (pg. 231) are smaller and have a narrow orange submarginal line on the ventral hindwing

Comments: This small but showy butterfly is primarily restricted to moist habitats where its weedy larval hosts occur. Adults nonetheless wander into adjacent drier sites in search of nectar. Like many wetland species, it has suffered from the loss or degradation of suitable habitat. The Bronze Copper tends to occur in small, localized colonies but can be fairly common when encountered. Males perch on low vegetation with their wings partially open, awaiting passing females.

Bronze Copper
Lycaena hyllus

Family/Subfamily: Gossamer Wings (Lycaenidae)/
Coppers (Lycaeninae)

Wingspan: 1.25–1.65" (3.2–4.2 cm)

Above: male is brown with purplish iridescence and a scalloped
orange submarginal band on hindwing; female has light
orange forewings with black spots and broad dark borders;
hindwing is purplish brown with a scalloped orange submarginal band on hindwing

Below: scattered white-rimmed black spots on wings; forewing
is orange with a light gray apex; hindwing is light gray with a
broad submarginal orange band containing black spots

Sexes: dissimilar; female has increased orange on dorsal
forewing and more-rounded wings

Egg: whitish, turban-shaped, laid singly on host stems or leaves

Larva: slug-like, yellow green with a darker green dorsal stripe

Larval Host Plants: knotweed (*Polygonum* spp.), Curly Dock
(*Rumex crispus*), and Greater Water Dock (*Rumex orbiculatus*)

Habitat: open, moist sites, including fens, wet meadows, and
marshes; also adjacent fields

Broods: typically one to two generations; eggs overwinter

Abundance: occasional to common

Range: throughout most of the region west to Nebraska and
the Dakotas

Freija Fritillary
Boloria freija

Family/Subfamily: Brush-Footed Butterflies (Nymphalidae)/ Fritillaries and Longwings (Heliconiinae)

Wingspan: 1.25–1.65" (3.2–4.2 cm)

Habitat: bogs and adjacent forest clearings and margins

Range: extreme northern counties of Minnesota, Michigan, and Wisconsin; rare to uncommon; very localized

Sexes: similar

Larva: blackish brown with light spots and short, black spines

Above: orange to light orange with black bands and spots; wing bases are dark with extensive black scaling

Below: hindwing is reddish brown to tawny with a complex pattern including a median and marginal row of white crescents capped in black; basal half of the hindwing has additional larger triangular or arrowhead-shaped white spots

Compare: Arctic Fritillary (pg. 235)

Comments: In our region, it occurs or has been documented from the far northern counties of the Upper Great Lakes. Adults are on the wing very early in the season.

Ottoe Skipper
Hesperia ottoe

Family/Subfamily: Skippers (Hesperiidae)/
Grass-Skippers (Hesperiinae)

Wingspan: 1.3–1.6" (3.3–4.1 cm)

Habitat: mixed and tallgrass prairie, barrens, and open areas

Range: scattered throughout; very rare and localized

Sexes: dissimilar; dorsal forewing in females is brown with pale dorsal forewing spots and no black stigma

Larva: pale green with tiny white spots, narrow lateral cream stripes, and a black head with orange spots around margin

Above: male is bright orange with narrow, diffuse wing borders and a black forewing stigma; female is brown with reduced orange scaling and several light forewing spots

Below: hindwing is clear yellow orange; occasionally with faint light postmedian spot band in females

Compare: Byssus Skipper (pg. 261)

Comments: A habitat specialist; populations are widely distributed and fragmented, being rare and declining to imperiled in many locations. Larvae utilize several native grasses.

ventral

Compare: Frigga Fritillary (pg. 256) has noticeably darker ventral wing bases and a large basal cream patch on the underside of the hindwing.

Comments: This species is arguably one of the most common lesser fritillaries across much of our region. It inhabits a variety of dry-to-wet open habitats, from alkaline fens to old fields, and is quite tolerant of disturbed landscapes. Because of its broader habitat tolerance, the Meadow Fritillary has not mirrored the declines of some other, more wetland-specialist members of the genus. Despite being relatively common, it tends not to be seen in large numbers. Adults often alight on low vegetation or on the ground with wings open.

Meadow Fritillary
Boloria bellona

Family/Subfamily: Brush-Footed Butterflies (Nymphalidae)/ Fritillaries and Longwings (Heliconiinae)

Wingspan: 1.25–1.9" (3.2–4.8 cm)

Above: orange with black bands and spots; wings are elongated and forewing apex is squared off

Below: hindwing is mottled brown and orange with violet frosting along the margin; lacks any silver spots

Sexes: similar

Egg: tiny, cream, cone-shaped, laid singly on or near host; often on other nearby plants

Larva: purplish black with some lighter markings and short, cream-based spines

Larval Host Plants: violets (*Viola* spp.)

Habitat: wet meadows, old fields, moist prairies, pastures, roadsides, and easements

Broods: two or more generations; larvae overwinter

Abundance: occasional to common

Range: northern two-thirds of the region

Compare: Pearl Crescent (pg. 247) and Northern Crescent (pg. 265) have more-extensive orange areas on the dorsal hindwing and a prominent dark marginal patch on the ventral hindwing

Comments: The Tawny Crescent is a generally uncommon and highly colonial species but can at times be locally more numerous. Because of its close resemblance to the more widespread and abundant Pearl and Northern Crescents, populations may be easily overlooked. In general, it tends to be found in slightly drier habitats that the others. Close examination of all adults in the field is recommended. Known populations should be monitored and conserved.

Tawny Crescent

Phyciodes batesii

Family/Subfamily: Brush-Footed Butterflies (Nymphalidae)/
True Brush-Foots (Nymphalinae)

Wingspan: 1.3–1.75" (3.3–4.4 cm)

Above: orange to tawny orange with black bands, spots, and
wing borders

Below: hindwing in male is mostly uniform golden yellow brown
with fine brown markings; lacks darker marginal hindwing
patch; hindwing has faint, pale marginal crescent; hindwing in
female has a somewhat more pronounced, darker marginal
patch enclosing pale crescent

Sexes: similar, although female has more extensive
dark markings

Egg: small, green, laid in clusters on the underside of host
plant's leaves

Larva: pinkish brown with a darker dorsal line and several rows
of short, branched spines

Larval Host Plants: various asters (*Symphyotrichum* spp. and
Eurybia spp.)

Habitat: dry woodland openings, barrens, pastures, hillsides,
margins and adjacent open fields, meadows, and roadsides

Broods: one generation; larvae overwinter

Abundance: rare to uncommon

Range: throughout the northern third of the region

Frigga Fritillary
Boloria frigga

Family/Subfamily: Brush-Footed Butterflies (Nymphalidae)/ Fritillaries and Longwings (Heliconiinae)

Wingspan: 1.4–1.75" (3.6–4.4 cm)

Habitat: bogs; occasionally swamps and other wet habitats

Range: extreme northern counties of Minnesota, Michigan, and Wisconsin; rare; very localized

Sexes: similar; female is often slightly paler with rounder wings

Larva: black with a purple lateral stripe and short, black spines

Above: dull orange with black bands and spots; wing bases are dark with extensive black scaling

Below: hindwing is brownish orange with somewhat dirty cream median spot band, a large elongated cream spot at the base along the leading margin, and extensive purplish frosting along the outer margin

Compare: Meadow Fritillary (pg. 253)

Comments: Within North America, it occurs across the Far North (Alaska and Canada) and just barely crosses the border south into the Upper Great Lakes states.

Bog Fritillary
Boloria eunomia

Family/Subfamily: Brush-Footed Butterflies (Nymphalidae)/ Fritillaries and Longwings (Heliconiinae)

Wingspan: 1.4–1.75" (3.6–4.4 cm)

Habitat: open bogs

Range: extreme northern parts of Minnesota, Wisconsin, and Michigan; rare to occasional; localized

Sexes: similar, although female is slightly paler with increased black scaling on dorsal wing bases

Larva: dark brown with reddish orange-based spines

Above: orange to tawny orange with heavy black bands and spots; broad black wing borders enclose small orange spots

Below: hindwing is reddish brown with basal, median, postmedian, and marginal rows of black-outlined white spots

Compare: Silver-Bordered Fritillary (pg. 269)

Comments: The Bog Fritillary is a handsome and widespread boreal species that just barely enters our region in the northernmost counties of the Upper Great Lakes states. As its name suggests, it is restricted to open bogs.

ventral

Compare: Gorgone Checkerspot (pg. 247) has a very complex ventral hindwing pattern with a median row of arrowhead-shaped white spots; dorsal, submarginal hindwing black spot band lacks any white centers; Harris's Checkerspot (pg. 260) has a complete row of similar-sized marginal white crescent spots on the ventral hindwing and is overall more orange below

Comments: This large checkerspot is widely distributed across the eastern US and southern Canada. Populations tend to fluctuate from year to year in many locations and are somewhat localized, especially in proximity to larval hosts. Nonetheless, the Silvery Checkerspot can often be quite abundant where found. The adults often gather in numbers at damp ground or animal dung. The young larvae feed gregariously when young, becoming more solitary with age. Partially grown larvae overwinter.

Silvery Checkerspot

Chlosyne nycteis

Family/Subfamily: Brush-Footed Butterflies (Nymphalidae)/
True Brush-Foots (Nymphalinae)

Wingspan: 1.4–2.0" (3.6–5.1 cm)

Above: tawny orange with black bands and broad black wing
borders; wing bases are heavily banded with black; hindwing
has a submarginal row of small (some white-centered) black
spots and a narrow black marginal line; wing fringes are
checkered in white

Below: hindwing is pale yellow brown with a darker brown
marginal patch enclosing a large, crescent-shaped cream
spot (part of an incomplete row of additional much
smaller crescents)

Sexes: similar, although female is somewhat larger

Egg: small, cream, laid in clusters on the underside of host
plant's leaves

Larva: dark brownish black with a wide orange lateral band and
several rows of short, branched black spines

Larval Host Plants: various aster family (Asteraceae) plants,
including Wingstem (*Verbesina alternifolia*), White Crown-
beard (*Verbesina virginica*), sunflower (*Helianthus* spp.),
coneflower (*Rudbeckia* spp.), and asters (*Eurybia* spp. and
Symphyotrichum spp.)

Habitat: rich woodland openings, margins and roadsides, stream
corridors, marshes, wet meadows, and fields

Broods: one to two generations; larvae overwinter

Abundance: uncommon to common

Range: throughout, although less common in western portions
of the region

Harris's Checkerspot
Chlosyne harrisii

Family/Subfamily: Brush-Footed Butterflies (Nymphalidae)/ True Brush-Foots (Nymphalinae)

Wingspan: 1.4–2.0" (3.6–5.1 cm)

Habitat: bogs, wet meadows, marshes, and other wetlands

Range: northern third of region; rare in western portions; uncommon to occasional; highly localized

Sexes: similar, although female is somewhat larger

Larva: reddish orange with black transverse stripes and several rows of short, branched black spines

Above: tawny orange with black bands and wing borders; wing bases are heavily banded with black; hindwing has a submarginal row of small black spots; wing fringes are checkered

Below: hindwing is reddish orange with three bands of white spots or crescents outlined in black; submarginal row of white crescents is complete and of overall uniform size

Compare: Silvery Checkerspot (pg. 259)

Comments: The species is considered vulnerable or of conservation concern in several states due to land-use changes.

Byssus Skipper
Problema byssus

Family/Subfamily: Skippers (Hesperiidae)/
Grass-Skippers (Hesperiinae)

Wingspan: 1.5–1.75" (3.6–4.6 cm)

Habitat: prairie

Range: western and central portions; rare to uncommon; local

Sexes: dissimilar; female dark brown with yellow-orange forewing spots; ventral hindwing more orange

Larva: green with a darker green dorsal stripe and a tan head
marked with reddish stripes

Above: male is somewhat variable; golden orange to orange
with dark brown to blackish borders, forewing has black cell-
end bar, often black scaling in the cell, no stigma, and slightly
darkened veins; female is dark brown; forewing has postmedian row of long yellow-orange spots and orange cell spots

Below: hindwing yellow orange to orange, narrow darker margin,
and postmedian band of lighter spots

Compare: Delaware Skipper (pg. 237)

Comments: Populations are fragmented and uncommon at best.

Compare: Indian Skipper (pg. 243) has yellow-orange ventral hindwing with pale-yellow spot band and flies in early summer; Common Branded Skipper (pg. 135) is very similar but has a strongly broken postmedian spot band on the ventral hindwing

Comments: The adults of this large, late-season skipper emerge in late summer and fly well into September or even early October in some locations. Two different-looking subspecies (previously considered separate species) occur in our region. Leonard's Skipper (subspecies *leonardus*) occurs throughout much of the eastern US and southeastern Canada. The Pawnee Skipper (subspecies *pawnee*), which is much lighter ventrally, occurs in western portions of our region and is imperiled throughout. Adults have a very strong flight but readily visit available flowers. Larvae construct nests at the base of grass clumps.

Leonard's Skipper

Hesperia leonardus

Family/Subfamily: Skippers (Hesperiidae)/
Banded Skippers (Hesperiinae)

Wingspan: 1.5–1.75" (3.8–4.4 cm)

Above: male orange with broad dark brown wing borders and
a black forewing stigma; female brown with orange basal
scaling and pale yellow-orange spots

Below: hindwing is reddish-brown with postmedian row of
cream spots

Sexes: dissimilar; male orange above with dark borders; female
brown with pale spots

Egg: cream, laid singly on or near host

Larva: olive green; black head marked with cream

Larval Host Plants: various grasses, including bentgrass (*Agrostis*
spp.), Little Bluestem (*Schizachyrium scoparium*), and
Switchgrass (*Panicum virgatum*)

Habitat: dry open woodlands, barrens, prairie, meadows, and
brushy fields

Broods: one generation; larvae overwinter

Abundance: rare to common

Range: throughout

Compare: Pearl Crescent (pg. 247) is very similar above but the hindwing less of a prominent open orange area; ventral hindwing has a large, dark marginal patch with a pale crescent in both sexes

Comments: Living up to its name, the Northern Crescent is one of the most frequently encountered crescents in northern portions of the region. It is extremely similar in appearance to the closely related and more widespread Pearl Crescent, which it typically replaces in northern counties. That said, in many instances the two species cannot be reliably separated in the field.

Northern Crescent

Phyciodes cocyta

Family/Subfamily: Brush-Footed Butterflies (Nymphalidae)/ True Brush-Foots (Nymphalinae)

Wingspan: 1.5–1.9" (3.8–4.8 cm)

Above: orange to tawny orange with black bands, spots, and wing borders; male has a large, open area of orange on the hindwing

Below: hindwing in male is golden yellow brown with fine brown markings and a large, dark marginal patch without a pale crescent; hindwing in female has increased dark markings and a dark marginal patch typically enclosing a pale crescent

Sexes: similar, although female has more-extensive dark hind-wing markings below and a pale marginal crescent

Egg: small, green, laid in clusters on the underside of host leaves

Larva: dark brown to charcoal with a darker dorsal line; lateral cream stripes; and several rows of short, branched spines

Larval Host Plants: various asters (*Symphyotrichum* spp.)

Habitat: glades, woodland openings, margins and adjacent open fields, meadows, and roadsides

Broods: one generation; larvae overwinter

Abundance: occasional to abundant

Range: throughout the northern third of the region

dorsal

Compare: unique; look for the long "snout"

Comments: The American Snout gets its odd name from its prominent and forward-pointing labial palpi, which resemble a long snout, beak, nose, or—with some imagination—a leaf petiole (stalk). This unique feature, combined with the cryptic coloration of the ventral hindwings, enhances the butterfly's overall "dead leaf" appearance when at rest. A resident of southern portions of the US, it regularly immigrates northward to temporarily colonize much of the Midwest and southern Ontario each year. Despite this, its presence is often sporadic, especially in more northerly portions of the region.

American Snout

Libytheana carinenta

Family/Subfamily: Brush-footed Butterflies (Nymphalidae)/ Snouts (Libytheinae)

Wingspan: 1.6–2.0" (4.1–5.0 cm)

Above: brown with orange patches and white spots near squared-off forewing apex

Below: forewing is brown with orange basal scaling and white spots near apex; hindwing is variable with bark-like pattern; hindwing underside is plain grayish brown or pinkish brown with mottling

Sexes: similar

Egg: tiny and white; laid in axils of host leaves

Larva: variable; light green with numerous yellow dots and a yellow lateral stripe; darker form has blackish longitudinal stripes; anterior portion has two small, black spots like false eyes

Larval Host Plants: Common Hackberry (*Celtis occidentalis*), Sugarberry (*Celtis laevigata*), and Dwarf Hackberry (*Celtis tenuifolia*)

Habitat: rich, deciduous woodlands, stream corridors, swamps, forest margins, woodland clearings, and adjacent open areas; wooded yards and neighborhoods

Broods: one or more generations; adults overwinter in southern portions of the US

Abundance: rare to common; sporadic

Range: throughout most of the region; rare or absent from the far north

ventral

Compare: Bog Fritillary (pg. 257) has a row of white—not black—submarginal spots on the ventral hindwing

Comments: This small species is named for its numerous silvery spot bands on the ventral hindwing. Primarily a denizen of open, moist habitats, it has declined in some locations due to the continued loss of wetlands. As a result, while the Silver-Bordered Fritillary is widespread, populations tend to be fairly localized. While often encountered as singletons or in small numbers, it can at times be fairly abundant. Adults have a rapid and somewhat erratic flight, typically low to the ground. They frequently pause to feed at available flowers or perch on low-growing vegetation.

Silver-Bordered Fritillary
Boloria selene

Family/Subfamily: Brush-Footed Butterflies (Nymphalidae)/ Fritillaries and Longwings (Heliconiinae)

Wingspan: 1.6–2.1" (4.1–5.3 cm)

Above: orange with black bands and spots; black wing borders enclose small orange spots

Below: hindwing is mottled reddish brown and tan with basal, median, postmedian, and marginal rows of black-outlined white spots and a row of small submarginal black spots

Sexes: similar

Egg: tiny, cream, cone-shaped, laid singly and somewhat haphazardly on or near host

Larva: dark gray with black patches, numerous orange spines, and two forward-pointing spines just behind the head

Larval Host Plants: violets (*Viola* spp.)

Habitat: wet meadows, moist prairies, sedge marshes, swamps, bogs, and adjacent fields and roadsides

Broods: two or more generations; larvae overwinter

Abundance: occasional to common; localized

Range: northern two-thirds of the region

Hoary Comma
Polygonia gracilis

Family/Subfamily: Brush-Footed Butterflies (Nymphalidae)/ True Brush-Foots (Nymphalinae)

Wingspan: 1.75–2.1" (4.4–5.3 cm)

Habitat: forests; woodland roads; trails

Range: extreme north and west; rare

Sexes: similar

Larva: black with many tiny white spots; orange dorsally; posterior dorsal portion is cream; rows of pale spines with orange bases

Above: tawny orange with black spots; irregular wing margins; forewing apex is extended and squared off; hindwing has a stubby tail; hindwing has a submarginal row of golden spots

Below: dark gray brown with heavy striations; bark-like appearance; two-toned with basal half darker and noticeably lighter gray outer half; hindwing has a central comma-shaped spot

Compare: Satyr Comma (opposite)

Comments: The Hoary Comma's close resemblance to similar species makes identification challenging.

Satyr Comma
Polygonia satyrus

Family/Subfamily: Brush-Footed Butterflies (Nymphalidae)/
True Brush-Foots (Nymphalinae)

Wingspan: 1.8–2.4" (4.6–6.1 cm)

Habitat: forests; woodland roads; trails

Range: extreme northern and western parts; rare to uncommon

Sexes: similar

Larva: black with a broad cream dorsal stripe, narrow cream
lateral stripe, and numerous branched, cream spines

Above: tawny orange to golden orange with black spots; irregular wing margins; forewing apex is extended and squared
off; hindwing has a short stubby tail, a pale margin with
dark submarginal line, and an adjacent inward golden line
or fused spot band

Below: mottled dark and light brown; hindwing has a darker
central band and comma-shaped spot

Compare: Hoary Comma (opposite) and Eastern Comma (pg. 281)

Comments: Named for the mythological woodland deity, it is
found in forest openings and margins.

ventral

Compare: Great Spangled Fritillary (pg. 295) and Aphrodite Fritillary (pg. 293) have large, conspicuous silvery spots on the ventral hindwing

Comments: The Variegated Fritillary is another southern species that wanders northward and establishes temporary breeding colonies into southern Canada. There is no evidence that this species can successfully overwinter in the region. As a result, numbers often fluctuate from year to year. It tends to be more sporadic and uncommon farther north. The species is an intermediate of sorts between longwings and fritillaries, as its larvae are able to utilize both passionflowers and violets as hosts. Adults tend to have a low, erratic flight and regularly alight on vegetation or to nectar at available flowers.

Variegated Fritillary
Euptoieta claudia

Family/Subfamily: Brush-Footed Butterflies (Nymphalidae)/ Fritillaries and Longwings (Heliconiinae)

Wingspan: 1.75–2.25" (4.4–5.7 cm)

Above: pale brownish orange with black markings, narrow light median band, and darker tawny-orange wing bases

Below: overall brown; forewing has basal orange scaling; hindwing is mottled with tan, cream, and dark brown

Sexes: similar, although female is larger and has broader wings

Egg: tiny, cream, cone-shaped, laid single on host leaves, flower buds, or tendrils

Larva: reddish orange with black-spotted white longitudinal stripes and black spines

Larval Host Plants: passionflowers (*Passiflora* spp.), including Purple Passionflower (*Passiflora incarnata*) and Yellow Passionflower (*Passiflora lutea*); also violets (*Viola* spp.)

Habitat: open, sunny sites; old fields; forest margins and clearings; roadsides; pastures; and utility easements

Broods: two or more generations; pupae overwinter

Abundance: rare to common

Range: throughout, although less frequent in northern portions

ventral

Compare: Painted Lady (pg. 277) has somewhat broader black markings above and has a postmedian row of four small pale eyespots outlined in black on the ventral hindwing

Comments: Although widespread, the American Lady is seldom found in large numbers. It has an affinity for virtually any open, sunny habitat that supports its herbaceous larval hosts, and it is fond of flowers. Like other members of the genus *Vanessa*, it is unlikely that this species can survive the winter in our region. As a result, it annually recolonizes our area from the south each spring. This results in varying abundance from year to year. Individual larvae construct quite conspicuous, somewhat bulbous, silken shelters on the host plant.

American Lady

Vanessa virginiensis

Family/Subfamily: Brush-Footed Butterflies (Nymphalidae)/ True Brush-Foots (Nymphalinae)

Wingspan: 1.75–2.4" (4.4–6.1 cm)

Above: orange with dark markings; forewing has a somewhat extended and squared-off black apex with several small white spots; hindwing has a postmedian row of small, blue-centered round black spots

Below: forewing has pinkish scaling on inner half; hindwing is brown with ornate agate-like pattern, two large eyespots, and a submarginal lavender band

Sexes: similar

Egg: small, pale green, barrel-shaped, laid singly on host leaves

Larva: variable; greenish yellow with narrow black bands or black with cream bands and numerous, red-based, branched spines; has a pair of prominent white spots on each segment

Larval Host Plants: various herbaceous plants in the aster family (Asteraceae), including Western Pearly Everlasting (*Anaphalis margaritacea*), pussytoes (*Antennaria* spp.), and cudweed (*Pseudognaphalium* spp.)

Habitat: open, disturbed sites; roadsides; old fields; meadows and pastures; easements; parks, yards, and gardens

Broods: two or more generations; adults overwinter

Abundance: occasional to common

Range: throughout the Midwest

ventral

Compare: American Lady (pg. 275) has somewhat less broad black markings above and has two large eyespots on the ventral hindwing

Comments: Unable to survive freezing temperatures, the Painted Lady typically overwinters in northern Mexico and annually recolonizes much of the US and Canada each year. As a result, its occurrence can be somewhat sporadic, with populations varying considerably in abundance from year to year. The species can occasionally have large outbreak years. Adults are quite fond of flowers and can be common garden visitors. The species has a cosmopolitan distribution and is considered the most widespread butterfly in the world. Larvae feed communally in silken webs when young before becoming more solitary with age.

Painted Lady
Vanessa cardui

Family/Subfamily: Brush-Footed Butterflies (Nymphalidae)/ True Brush-Foots (Nymphalinae)

Wingspan: 1.75–2.4" (4.4–6.1 cm)

Above: pinkish orange with dark markings; forewing apex is black with several small white spots; hindwing has a post-median row of small, blue-centered, round black spots

Below: forewing has pinkish scaling on inner half; hindwing is brown with cream patches forming an ornate pattern, postmedian row of four pale-outlined, round black spots with blue centers, and a submarginal row of elongated lavender spots

Sexes: similar

Egg: small, pale green, barrel-shaped, laid singly on host leaves

Larva: variable; greenish yellow with black mottling to charcoal with cream mottling, yellow lateral spots, and several rows of branched spines

Larval Host Plants: various plants in several families (primarily Asteraceae, Malvaceae, and Boraginaceae), including thistle (*Cirsium* spp.)

Habitat: virtually any open habitat, including disturbed sites, roadsides, old fields, meadows, pastures, easements, parks, yards, and gardens

Broods: two or more generations; adults overwinter

Abundance: occasional to common

Range: throughout

Compare: Gray Comma (pg. 283) and Eastern Comma (pg. 281) both lack ventral rows of green spots and have less-jagged wing margins

Comments: This boldly patterned and somewhat reclusive boreal forest species is named for the small, iridescent green spots on the wings below. While distinctive, they can at times be hard to see, especially in older individuals. Like other anglewings, the adults hibernate over the winter in protected sites and may be temporarily active on warm early-spring days.

Green Comma

Polygonia faunus

Family/Subfamily: Brush-Footed Butterflies (Nymphalidae)/ True Brush-Foots (Nymphalinae)

Wingspan: 1.8–2.4" (4.6–6.1 cm)

Above: tawny orange with bold black spots and wing borders; very jagged wing margins; forewing apex is extended and squared off; hindwing has a short stubby tail; forewing has a smaller secondary dot just above larger black median spot near the training margin; hindwing has a submarginal band of small golden spots

Below: heavily mottled dark and light brown; bark-like appearance; two-toned appearance with darker basal half and lighter outer half; hindwing has postmedian and submarginal rows of small, iridescent green spots

Sexes: similar

Egg: small, green, barrel-shaped, laid singly on host leaves

Larva: black with a broad cream dorsal stripe, narrow orange lateral stripes, and numerous branched, cream spines

Larval Host Plants: Prairie Willow (*Salix humilis*), gooseberry (*Ribes* spp.), alder (*Alnus* spp.), and birch (*Betula* spp.)

Habitat: coniferous and mixed-hardwood forests, woodland roads, and trails and margins

Broods: one generation; adults overwinter

Abundance: rare to uncommon

Range: northernmost counties

ventral

Compare: Question Mark (pg. 287) is somewhat larger and has a central silver question mark-shaped spot on the ventral hindwing; Gray Comma (pg. 283) is very dark ventrally; Satyr Comma (pg. 271) is rare, found only in northernmost areas, and has light dorsal hindwing borders and tends to be paler ventrally; Green Comma (pg. 279) has somewhat more jagged wing margins and occur only in northernmost areas

Comments: This widespread species is arguably the most common comma in the region. That said, it is seldom seen in large numbers and can be easily confused with other members of the genus, so close observation is often needed to render a correct identification. The spiny larvae construct individual leaf shelters on the host by folding over leaves with silk. They stay inside during the day for protection and come out at night to feed. Late-season adults overwinter in protected sites.

Eastern Comma

Polygonia comma

Family/Subfamily: Brush-Footed Butterflies (Nymphalidae)/ True Brush-Foots (Nymphalinae)

Wingspan: 2.0–2.4" (5.1–6.1 cm)

Above: tawny orange with black spots; irregular wing margins; forewing apex is extended and squared off; hindwing has a short, stubby tail; summer-form hindwing is primarily black; cool-season form is primarily tawny orange with a submarginal row of golden spots

Below: variable; dead-leaf appearance; heavily banded with dark and light brown; cool-season forms are a more uniform brown; hindwing has a small, central, comma-shaped spot

Sexes: similar

Egg: small, green, barrel-shaped, laid singly or in small stacks on the underside of host leaves or stems

Larva: variable; black with cream to greenish-gray markings with darker markings and orange spots; numerous rows of pale, branched spines

Larval Host Plants: Smallspike False Nettle (*Boehmeria cylindrica*), Canada Wood Nettle (*Laportea canadensis*), Stinging Nettle (*Urtica dioica*), and Common Hop (*Humulus lupulus*); also elm (*Ulmus* spp.)

Habitat: deciduous and mixed forests, woodland openings, trails, and margins; parks, yards, and neighborhoods

Broods: two generations; adults overwinter

Abundance: occasional to common

Range: throughout, although less common in western portions of the region

Compare: Eastern Comma (pg. 281) is a somewhat lighter brown below, has less jagged wing margins, and has a more pronounced central silver comma on ventral hindwing; Satyr Comma (pg. 271) is rare, found only in northernmost areas, has light dorsal hindwing borders, and tends to be paler ventrally; Green Comma (pg. 279) has somewhat more jagged wing margins and only occurs in northernmost areas

Comments: This small woodland butterfly is aptly named for its dark-gray and highly striated ventral wings that closely resemble tree bark. Although widespread, it is seldom common and most often seen in smaller numbers or as singletons. Like other members of the genus, adult Gray Commas have a quick, erratic flight but readily perch on sunlit branches, rocks, or bare ground, where they are wary of close approach.

Gray Comma
Polygonia progne

Family/Subfamily: Brush-Footed Butterflies (Nymphalidae)/ True Brush-Foots (Nymphalinae)

Wingspan: 2.0–2.4" (5.1–6.1 cm)

Above: tawny orange with black spots and heavy black borders; irregular wing margins; forewing apex is extended and squared off; hindwing has a short, stubby tail; summer-form hindwing is primarily black with two small black spots on the leading margin; cool-season form primarily tawny orange with a submarginal row of golden spots

Below: dark gray brown with heavy striations; bark-like appearance; somewhat two-toned with basal half much darker; hindwing has a small, thin, central comma-shaped spot

Sexes: similar

Egg: small, green, barrel-shaped, laid singly or in small stacks on host leaves

Larva: yellow brown with black markings on each segment and numerous rows of pale, branched spines

Larval Host Plants: gooseberry (*Ribes* spp.)

Habitat: deciduous and mixed forests, woodland openings, trails, and margins; parks, yards, and neighborhoods

Broods: two generations; adults overwinter

Abundance: uncommon to occasional

Range: throughout, although less common in western portions of the region

ventral

Compare: Question Mark (pg. 287) is smaller and has irregular wing margins, extensive dark dorsal markings, and a squared-off forewing apex

Comments: This distinctive butterfly is named for one of its primary larval host plants (Goatweed, also called Hogwort). Although brilliantly orange in flight, its realistic leaf-like pattern below offers superb camouflage when at rest. A resident of the Deep South, the Goatweed Leafwing is mostly encountered in Missouri and southern Illinois, but rarely northward. It is a rare stray to the Upper Midwest. Individuals produced late in the season overwinter and reproduce in spring. Adults have a strong, powerful flight and readily perch with wings closed on tree trunks, branches, or on the ground. It does not visit flowers but instead prefers fermenting fruit and tree sap.

Goatweed Leafwing

Anaea andria

Family/Subfamily: Brush-Footed Butterflies (Nymphalidae)/ Leafwings (Charaxinae)

Wingspan: 2.25–3.0" (5.7–7.6 cm)

Above: forewing has a pointed apex; male is unmarked, bright reddish orange with narrow brown wing borders; female is lighter orange with dark markings, broader brown wing borders, and a pale, irregular postmedian band through both wings; hindwing has a pointed tail

Below: seasonally variable; dead-leaf pattern; light brownish gray to darker reddish brown; winter form has more pronounced hooked forewing apex and longer hindwing tail

Sexes: similar, although females are lighter and more heavily patterned

Egg: gray green, round, laid singly or in small groups on the underside of host leaves

Larva: gray green with numerous small white spots; head is gray with small, knobby orange bumps

Larval Host Plants: Hogwort (*Croton capitatus*) and Prairie Tea (*Croton monanthogynus*)

Habitat: dry woodland clearings, margins, and adjacent open sites

Broods: one or more generations; adults overwinter

Abundance: rare to occasional; local

Range: southern portion of the region; temporary colonist or rare stray northward

cool season

ventral

Compare: Eastern Comma (pg. 281) is smaller, with a less prominent hindwing tail and a comma-shaped silver spot in the center of the ventral hindwing; Gray Comma (pg. 283) is smaller, has a less prominent hindwing tail and a darker, more striated bark-like pattern below

Comments: This large anglewing gets its unique name from the small silvery spots on the underside of the hindwing, which resemble, with some imagination, the namesake punctuation mark. Generally common in a wide variety of forested habitats and adjacent open areas, it is seldom encountered in large numbers. Adults have strong, quick flight and are quite wary of close approach. They feed on rotting fruit, animal dung, urine, carrion, and sap flows but do occasionally visit flowers as well. Males perch on overhanging branches, tree trunks, or other objects to wait for females and regularly fly out at passing organisms.

Question Mark
Polygonia interrogationis

Family/Subfamily: Brush-Footed Butterflies (Nymphalidae)/ True Brush-Foots (Nymphalinae)

Wingspan: 2.25–3.0" (5.7–7.6 cm)

Above: orange with black spots and dark borders; forewing apex is squared off and hooked; hindwing is seasonally variable; summer form is mostly black; cool-season form is orange with black spots; wing edges have lavender edges, most noticeable in cool-season forms; hindwing has a short tail

Below: seasonally variable; dead-leaf pattern; brown to darker pinkish brown; hindwing has two small, median silvery spots that form a question mark shape.

Sexes: similar

Egg: small, green, barrel-shaped, laid singly or in small groups, one on top of the other on host leaves

Larva: variable; gray to black with cream stripes and spots, orange stripes, and numerous yellow-to-orange branched spines; the spines on the anterior and posterior region are black; head is reddish

Larval Host Plants: hackberry (*Celtis* spp.), elm (*Ulmus* spp.), false nettle (*Boehmeria* spp.), and nettle (*Urtica* spp.)

Habitat: deciduous forests and adjacent open areas, wooded trails, openings and margins, parks, and yards

Broods: two generations; adults overwinter

Abundance: occasional to common

Range: throughout, although less common to absent in far northwest portions of the region

Atlantis Fritillary
Speyeria atlantis

Family/Subfamily: Brush-Footed Butterflies (Nymphalidae)/ Fritillaries and Longwings (Heliconiinae)

Wingspan: 2.4–2.75" (6.1–7.0 cm)

Habitat: woodlands, trails, and roadsides

Range: northern and western parts of our region; occasional to common

Sexes: similar; female is usually larger and more golden orange

Larva: dark brown with fine yellowish striations, black blotches, a black dorsal stripe outlined in yellow, and numerous orange-brown spines

Above: orange with black spots and bands; wing margins have a broad, black border

Below: hindwing is dark purplish brown with metallic silver spots and a narrow, yellowish-tan submarginal band

Compare: Aphrodite Fritillary (pg. 293) and Great Spangled Fritillary (pg. 295)

Comments: Often the most common member of the genus when encountered. Adults have a strong flight and visit flowers.

Gulf Fritillary
Agraulis vanillae

Family/Subfamily: Brush-Footed Butterflies (Nymphalidae)/ Fritillaries and Longwings (Heliconiinae)

Wingspan: 2.5–3.75" (6.4–9.5 cm)

Habitat: open, sunny sites; fields, gardens, and parks

Range: extreme southern portions of the region; rare stray northward; rare to uncommon

Sexes: similar, although female often tawnier in color above

Larva: orange with black branched spines

Above: elongated wings are bright to tawny orange with black spots; forewing has three white-centered black spots; hindwing has a black chain-like pattern along outer margin

Below: hindwing is orange brown with elongated silvery spots

Compare: Viceroy (pg. 291) and Monarch (pg. 299)

Comments: Primarily a butterfly of the Deep South, the Gulf Fritillary expands its range northward to temporarily colonize extreme southern portions of our region each year. It is unable to survive freezing temperatures.

ventral

Compare: Monarch (pg. 299) is larger, is not confined to wetlands, and it lacks the black postmedian line through the hindwing

Comments: Widespread across our region and much of the US and southern Canada, the Viceroy is found in and near wetlands or moist sites that support its larval hosts. As a result, it tends to be fairly localized but can be quite common when found. Males regularly perch on overhanging branches awaiting passing females and dart out to investigate larger insects that pass by. Although once thought to be a palatable mimic of the toxic Monarch, studies have shown that both species are actually distasteful to certain predators. Adults visit a variety of food sources, including flower nectar, rotting fruit, dung, and even carrion.

Viceroy
Limenitis archippus

Family/Subfamily: Brush-Footed Butterflies (Nymphalidae)/ Admirals (Limenitidinae)

Wingspan: 2.6–3.2" (6.6–8.1 cm)

Above: orange with black wing veins and broad, black wing borders; borders contain small white spots; forewing has a partial black postmedian band with white spots; hindwing has a thin, black postmedian line

Below: as above but lighter orange in color; hindwing and forewing apex are often yellow orange

Sexes: similar

Egg: gray green, laid singly on the tips of host leaves

Larva: mottled green, brown, and cream with two long, knobby horns off the thorax; some larvae are browner; resembles a bird dropping

Larval Host Plants: primarily willow (*Salix* spp.); also poplar, aspen, and cottonwood (*Populus* spp.)

Habitat: shrubby wetlands, stream and pond margins, roadsides, ditches, swamps, wet meadows, and other consistently moist sites

Broods: two or more generations; larvae overwinter

Abundance: occasional to common; localized

Range: throughout

Compare: Great Spangled Fritillary (pg. 295) is larger, is more common, and has a broad yellow submarginal band on the ventral hindwing; Atlantis Fritillary (pg. 288) has a noticeably dark dorsal wing border

Comments: This widespread northern species tends to be associated more with wet and forested habitats than the Great Spangled Fritillary, with which it is easily confused. As a result, the Aphrodite Fritillary tends to occur in more-localized populations but still may be quite common when encountered. Adults are also less likely to wander far from suitable habitat in search of nectar. A patrolling species, males actively search for females, often following long, circuitous routes. Evidence suggests that climate warming is adversely affecting this species in some locations.

Aphrodite Fritillary
Speyeria aphrodite

Family/Subfamily: Brush-Footed Butterflies (Nymphalidae)/ Fritillaries and Longwings (Heliconiinae)

Wingspan: 2.7–3.3" (6.9–8.4 cm)

Above: orange with heavy black lines and spots; basal portions of wings are tawny in females

Below: variable; hindwing is a dark orange brown to reddish brown with numerous large, metallic silver spots and a narrow, yellowish submarginal band; band may be faint, reduced, or absent

Sexes: similar, although female is slightly paler above with darker, more tawny wing bases

Egg: tiny, cream, cone-shaped, laid singly and somewhat haphazardly on or near hosts

Larva: velvety black with several rows of branched, black spines; lateral two rows of spines are reddish brown with black tips

Larval Host Plants: violets (*Viola* spp.)

Habitat: open deciduous woodland, glades, forest clearings and margins, wet meadows and prairies, bogs, and roadsides

Broods: one generation; young larvae overwinter

Abundance: rare to occasional; locally common

Range: primarily the northern half of the region

ventral

Compare: Aphrodite Fritillary (pg. 293) is smaller, is less common, and has a narrower yellow submarginal band on the ventral hindwing

Comments: Easily the most conspicuous and widespread fritillary in the Midwest. It is not nearly as localized and habitat restricted as other members of the genus. Adults have a strong flight but frequently stop at available flowers, being particularly fond of milkweeds, thistles, and beebalms. It is not unusual to see several adults clustering on a single flower. The butterfly has a single long flight that extends from June to late September or even later. Males emerge weeks ahead of females, which begin laying eggs late in the season. The tiny, newly hatched larvae overwinter and complete development the following spring.

Great Spangled Fritillary
Speyeria cybele

Family/Subfamily: Brush-Footed Butterflies (Nymphalidae)/ Fritillaries and Longwings (Heliconiinae)

Wingspan: 2.9–3.8" (7.1–9.7 cm)

Above: orange with heavy black lines and spots; basal portions of wings are noticeably darker

Below: hindwing is dark orange brown to brownish with numerous large, metallic silver spots and a broad, yellowish submarginal band

Sexes: similar, although female is a paler golden orange above with darker wing bases

Egg: tiny, cream, cone-shaped, laid singly and somewhat haphazardly on or near hosts

Larva: velvety black with several rows of reddish-orange-based black, branched spines

Larval Host Plants: various violets (*Viola* spp.)

Habitat: open deciduous woodland, forest clearings and margins, old fields, meadows, prairies, roadsides, and easements

Broods: one generation; young larvae overwinter

Abundance: occasional to abundant

Range: throughout

ventral

Regal Fritillary
Speyeria idalia

Family/Subfamily: Brush-Footed Butterflies (Nymphalidae)/ Fritillaries and Longwings (Heliconiinae)

Wingspan: 3.1–4.0" (7.9–10.2 cm)

Habitat: grassy prairies, moist meadows, and grasslands

Range: throughout except in Ohio and Michigan; rare, localized

Sexes: similar, although female is larger and has all-white spots on dorsal hindwing

Larva: gray black; ochre-yellow to reddish-orange dorsal band and lateral mottling; dorsal spines are silvery white with black tips; lateral spines have orange bases; head is reddish

Above: forewing is reddish orange with black markings and white apical spots; hindwing is black with a bluish cast

Below: hindwing is dark brown with numerous, black-edged white (not silvery) spots

Compare: unique

Comments: This butterfly has declined significantly due to the loss of habitat. Today, it is a powerful flagship for prairie conservation.

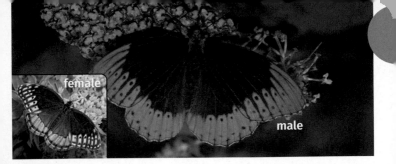

female

male

Diana Fritillary
Speyeria diana

Family/Subfamily: Brush-Footed Butterflies (Nymphalidae)/ Fritillaries and Longwings (Heliconiinae)

Wingspan: 3.6–4.5" (9.1–11.4 cm)

Habitat: woodlands, roadsides, and stream margins

Range: southern Missouri and Kentucky; rare to uncommon

Sexes: dissimilar; male is orange and black; female is black and blue and often much larger

Larva: fleshy black with rows of orange-based spines

Above: dimorphic; male has blackish-brown wings with orange margins; female has black wings with broad blue hindwing margins; forewing margin has blue and/or white spots

Below: male hindwing is orange; female hindwing is brown

Compare: Red-Spotted Purple (pg. 43); Pipevine Swallowtail (pg. 41)

Comments: This butterfly is impressive in size and appearance. Females mimic the toxic Pipevine Swallowtail. Populations are declining. The larvae utilize various violets (*Viola* spp.) as hosts.

ventral

Compare: Viceroy (pg. 291) is smaller and has a prominent black postmedian line through the hindwing

Comments: The Monarch is arguably the most popular and widely recognized butterfly in North America. During spring and summer, Monarchs breed throughout the US and southern Canada. In the fall, adults from the larger eastern population migrate to Mexico, flying up to 3,000 miles. This annual fall mass migration is one of the greatest natural events undertaken by any organism on Earth. The conspicuous striped larvae feed on various milkweed species and sequester toxic compounds called cardenolides, which render them and the resulting adults unpalatable to various vertebrate predators. Unfortunately, Monarch populations have decreased significantly over the past several decades, resulting in conservation efforts to help rebuild their breeding habitat.

Monarch
Danaus plexippus

Family/Subfamily: Brush-Footed Butterflies (Nymphalidae)/ Milkweed Butterflies (Danainae)

Wingspan: 3.5–4.0" (8.9–10.2 cm)

Above: orange with black veins and wing borders; black borders have two rows of small, white spots; male has a small, black androcolonial scent patch in center of hindwing

Below: as above but lighter in coloration

Sexes: similar, although female is often tawnier and lacks black hindwing scent patch

Egg: white, cone-shaped, laid singly on host leaves, flower buds, or flowers

Larva: white with transverse yellow and black stripes; pair of thin, black filaments off each end

Larval Host Plants: various milkweeds (*Asclepias* spp.)

Habitat: open, sunny locations, including old fields, roadsides, meadows, prairies, agricultural land, parks, and gardens; may be found in virtually any habitat during fall migration

Broods: two or more generations; overwinter as adults in Mexico

Abundance: occasional to common

Range: throughout most of the region

Compare: Olympia Marble (pg. 307) has a charcoal forewing apex, lacks orange forewing apex in males, and has yellow-green marbling on ventral hindwing; found in drier habitats

Comments: The Falcate Orangetip is a small, early-season butterfly of open, often-mesic woodlands and margins. While the forewings are noticeably hooked in both sexes, only males have prominent bright-orange forewing tips. The resulting color pattern is quite noticeable even in a somewhat shade-dappled forest understory. Adults have a quick, low flight. Males actively patrol in search of females.

Falcate Orangetip

Anthocharis midea

Family/Subfamily: Whites and Sulphurs (Pieridae)/
Whites (Pierinae)

Wingspan: 1.0–1.75" (2.54–4.54 cm)

Above: male is white with black-and-white-checkered wing
border, orange forewing apex, and black forewing cell spot;
female is like male but lacks orange forewing apex; both
sexes have hooked forewing tip

Below: hindwing is white with gray-green, marble-like pattern

Sexes: dissimilar; female lacks orange forewing apex

Egg: orange, spindle-shaped, laid singly on host plant

Larva: green to blue green with lateral white stripes, a yellow-
orange dorsal stripe, and numerous small, black dots

Larval Host Plants: wild members of the mustard family
(Brassicaceae), including toothwort (*Cardamine* spp.) and
rockcress (*Arabis* spp.)

Habitat: open woodlands, forest borders, and stream margins

Broods: one generation

Abundance: uncommon to occasional; locally common

Range: extreme southern portions of the region

Compare: Cabbage White (pg. 313) has black wing tips, has one or two black forewing spots, and inhabits open habitats. Mustard White (pg. 305) has yellow at the base of the ventral hindwing and darker scaling along the wing veins.

Comments: A small, ghostly butterfly of early spring, it is uncommon and declining throughout much of its range. Unlike most other members of the family, the West Virginia White is primarily restricted to wooded habitats. It is often highly localized in occurrence and a poor pioneer species, with adults reluctant to cross large, open expanses. The spread of invasive Garlic Mustard threatens populations. While female butterflies lay eggs on the plant, the developing larvae are typically unable to successfully complete development. Adults have a low, weak flight and maneuver slowly along the forest floor.

West Virginia White

Pieris virginiensis

Family/Subfamily: Whites and Sulphurs (Pieridae)/ Whites (Pierinae)

Wingspan: 1.2–1.6" (3.0–4.1 cm)

Above: unmarked white to smoky white with black scaling along the costal margin and wing bases

Below: hindwings are white with brown scaling along veins

Sexes: similar, but female typically looks smokier white above

Egg: greenish white, spindle-shaped, laid singly on underside of host leaves

Larva: gray green with longitudinal yellow-orange stripes, numerous small black dots, and short hairs

Larval Host Plants: toothworts (*Cardamine* spp.)

Habitat: moist, deciduous woodlands and mixed forests; forest margins and occasionally adjacent semiopen areas

Broods: one generation; pupae overwinter

Abundance: uncommon to occasional; highly localized

Range: eastern portions of the region

Compare: Cabbage White (pg. 313) has black wing tips and single or double round, black forewing spot; West Virginia White (pg. 303) lacks a yellow patch at hindwing base and a single spring flight

Comments: Aptly named, the Mustard White uses various plants in the mustard family as larval hosts. Widespread across northern portions of the Midwest from the eastern Dakotas to northern Ohio and southern Ontario, it is a butterfly of woodlands and adjacent open habitats. Unlike the spring-flying West Virginia White, with which it may be easily confused, the Mustard White produces two generations found from early spring to mid-fall. Like the West Virginia White, it is negatively impacted by the invasive Garlic Mustard, which outcompetes native hosts and hinders larval survival.

Mustard White
Pieris oleracea

Family/Subfamily: Whites and Sulphurs (Pieridae)/ Whites (Pierinae)

Wingspan: 1.2–2.25" (3.0–5.7 cm)

Above: seasonally variable; spring form is white with charcoal scaling at wing bases and forewing tip; summer form is immaculate white or has a slight dusting of charcoal along costal margin

Below: hindwings seasonally variable; spring form is white with pale yellowish cast and veins crisply outlined in gray green; summer form is immaculate white; both forms have a yellow patch at hindwing base

Sexes: similar

Egg: greenish white, spindle-shaped, laid singly on host leaves or stems

Larva: green with small black spots and short hairs

Larval Host Plants: various mustards (Brassicaceae), including rockcress (*Arabis* spp.) and bittercress (*Cardamine* spp.)

Habitat: moist, deciduous woodlands; forest margins; brushy wetlands; and adjacent moist meadows

Broods: two generations; pupae overwinter in warmer climates

Abundance: occasional to locally common

Range: primarily northern portions of the region; uncommon or absent farther south

Compare: Large Marble (pg. 311) is larger, has more ventral hind-wing marbling, and has a very limited range within region

Comments: An early-season species, the Olympia Marble can often be spotted on sunny spring days. Although widespread, populations tend to be quite localized but often support sizable numbers when encountered. The small, delicate-looking adults maneuver close to the ground with a direct and somewhat rapid flight. While frequently visiting flowers, they are quite skittish and often difficult to closely approach.

Olympia Marble
Euchloe olympia

Family/Subfamily: Whites and Sulphurs (Pieridae)/ Whites (Pierinae)

Wingspan: 1.25–1.75" (3.2–4.54 cm)

Above: white with black scaling at bases; forewing has a charcoal apex and black cell bar

Below: hindwing is white with yellow-green marbling; fresh adults have a pinkish flush near the base of the hindwing

Sexes: similar

Egg: white, spindle-shaped, laid singly on host leaves or on flower buds

Larva: gray green with longitudinal yellow stripes, a yellow-and-white lateral stripe, and numerous small black dots

Larval Host Plants: wild members of the mustard family (Brassicaceae), including rockcress (*Arabis* spp.)

Habitat: open semiarid habitats, including barrens, dry open woodlands, dry meadows, and lakeshore dunes

Broods: one generation; pupae overwinter

Abundance: rare to occasional; locally common

Range: sporadic throughout much of the region

Compare: Cabbage White (pg. 313) has black wing tips and single or double round, black forewing spot; Mustard White (pg. 305) has a more-continuous black forewing spot band

Comments: A sporadic or infrequent seasonal colonist throughout much of the region, it tends to be more abundant in the southern and western portions of the US. As a result, its presence and population numbers often fluctuate considerably from year to year, being most numerous late in the growing season. Populations are unlikely to survive harsh winters in most portions of the Midwest. Adults have a quick, erratic flight that is often low to the ground, and they can be a challenge to closely approach.

Checkered White
Pontia protodice

Family/Subfamily: Whites and Sulphurs (Pieridae)/ Whites (Pierinae)

Wingspan: 1.25–2.0" (3.2–5.1 cm)

Above: male is white with charcoal markings on forewing and unmarked hindwing; female is grayish white with extensive charcoal markings on both wings

Below: hindwings are white with grayish markings and yellow-green scaling along veins; spring form features darker scaling along veins

Sexes: similar, although female is more heavily marked

Egg: yellow, spindle-shaped, laid singly on host leaves and flowers

Larva: gray; longitudinal yellow-orange stripes; black dots; short hairs

Larval Host Plants: various mustards (Brassicaceae), including Virgina Pepperweed (*Lepidium virginicum*) and Shepherd's Purse (*Capsella bursa-pastoris*)

Habitat: open, disturbed sites, including fallow agricultural fields, old fields, and roadsides

Broods: two or more generations; pupae overwinter in warmer climates

Abundance: rare to occasional

Range: primarily southern portions of the region; uncommon or absent farther north

Compare: Olympia Marble (pg. 307) is smaller, has less ventral hindwing marbling, and is more widespread

Comments: The Large Marble and other members of the genus Euchloe are named for their distinctive ventral hindwing pattern. Although widespread and often locally common throughout the Mountain West, it extends into eastern North America in a fairly narrow band along southern Canada and the Upper Great Lakes to south-central Ontario. Midwest records are quite limited.

Large Marble
Euchloe ausonides

Family/Subfamily: Whites and Sulphurs (Pieridae)/ Whites (Pierinae)

Wingspan: 1.4–2.0" (3.6–5.1 cm)

Above: white with black scaling at bases; forewing has a charcoal-patterned apex and black cell bar

Below: white; forewing apex has greenish scaling; hindwing is white with extensive greenish marbling and yellow-lined veins

Sexes: similar, although dorsal hindwings often have a some-what yellow cast in females

Egg: greenish white, spindle-shaped, laid singly on host flower buds

Larva: bluish gray with longitudinal yellow stripes, a yellow-and-white lateral stripe, and numerous small black dots

Larval Host Plants: wild members of the mustard family (Brassicaceae), including rockcress (*Arabis* spp.) and Tall Tumble Mustard (*Sisymbrium altissimum*)

Habitat: forest openings and trails, rock outcroppings, hillsides, and ridgetops

Broods: one generation; pupae overwinter

Abundance: rare and very localized

Range: restricted to extreme western South Dakota, northern Minnesota, and Isle Royale in the Upper Peninsula of Michigan

ventral

Compare: Checkered White (pg. 309) has extensive black checkered pattern; Mustard White (pg. 305) and West Virginia White (pg. 303) lack black forewing tip, black forewing spots, and prefer more-wooded habitats

Comments: Accidentally introduced from Europe around 1860, the Cabbage White quickly radiated across much of North America. It is widespread across the Midwest and southern Canada. Adults are often encountered in vegetable gardens, where the larvae feed on cabbage, broccoli, cauliflower, and other cultivated mustard plants. As a result, it is one of the few butterfly species considered to be an agricultural and garden pest. Adults have a somewhat slow, fluttering flight and are easy to closely observe.

Cabbage White
Pieris rapae

Family/Subfamily: Whites and Sulphurs (Pieridae)/
Whites (Pierinae)

Wingspan: 1.5–2.0" (3.8–5.1 cm)

Above: white with black forewing tips; male has a single black
postmedian spot on forewing; female has two black spots

Below: as above, but forewing tip is yellow; hindwing is creamy
yellow with some scattered black scaling

Sexes: similar, although female has two black forewing spots

Egg: white, spindle-shaped, laid singly on host leaves
and flowers

Larva: green with small lateral yellow dashes, yellow dorsal
stripe, and numerous short hairs

Larval Host Plants: wild and cultivated members of the mustard
family (Brassicaceae)

Habitat: open, disturbed sites, including agricultural fields, old
fields, roadsides, weedy lots, yards, and gardens; occasionally
open woodland

Broods: multiple generations

Abundance: occasional to abundant

Range: throughout the region

Compare: unique

Comments: A spectacular species, the long-tailed, black-and-white–striped Zebra Swallowtail cannot be confused with any other butterfly in the region. It is most abundant across southern portions of Ohio, Indiana, Illinois, Missouri, and eastern Kansas and is quite uncommon or absent farther north. Adults have a somewhat low, rapid flight and adeptly maneuver through the forest understory or adjacent more open sites. Seldom found far from populations of its larval host, the Zebra Swallowtail is unlikely to be encountered in more-urbanized locations but may occasionally wander into nearby gardens. It has a proportionately short proboscis and is unable to feed at longer, more tubular blossoms. It instead prefers more-compact blooms and is fond of white-flowered species. Males often gather at moist ground.

Zebra Swallowtail

Eurytides marcellus

Family/Subfamily: Swallowtails (Papilionidae)/
Swallowtails (Papilioninae)

Wingspan: 2.5–4.0" (6.4–10.2 cm)

Above: white with black stripes and a single long hindwing tail;
hindwing has a bright-red patch above the eyespot; spring
individuals are smaller, lighter in color, and have shorter tails

Below: as above, but with a distinctive red stripe through
the hindwing

Sexes: similar

Egg: light green, round, laid singly on host plant's leaves or
budding branches

Larva: several color forms; may be green, green with light-blue
and yellow stripes, or charcoal with white and yellow stripes

Larval Host Plants: Pawpaw (*Asimina triloba*)

Habitat: moist, deciduous woodlands; forest openings; stream
corridors; forest edges and adjacent clearings; roadsides; and
occasionally gardens

Broods: two; pupae overwinter

Abundance: rare to common

Range: primarily southern third of the region; absent, rare, or
uncommon farther north

Compare: Little Yellow (pg. 319) is larger and has rounder wings; dorsal forewing lacks black bar along training edge; ventral forewing lacks black dots and orange scaling along leading edge

Comments: As its name implies, the Dainty Sulphur is the smallest sulphur in the region. A resident of the Deep South, it strays or temporarily colonizes many more-northern locations each year, more often being encountered in late summer or early fall. Adults have a low, erratic flight. This behavior, combined with its small size, makes the butterfly relatively easy to overlook.

Dainty Sulphur

Nathalis iole

Family/Subfamily: Whites and Sulphurs (Pieridae)/ Sulphurs (Coliadinae)

Wingspan: 0.75–1.25" (1.9–3.2 cm)

Above: lemon yellow with black forewing tips and a black bar along inner margin of forewing; female has orange-yellow hindwings and more extensive black scaling

Below: hindwing is yellow with greenish-black markings; seasonally variable; cool-season individuals are more heavily pigmented; forewing has orange scaling along leading edge and black spots

Sexes: similar, although black markings are more extensive on females

Egg: yellow, spindle-shaped, laid singly on host leaves

Larva: green with thin, lateral yellow and lavender stripes

Larval Host Plants: Green Carpetweed (*Mollugo verticillata*), Common Sneezeweed (*Helenium autumnale*), and White Beggarticks (*Bidens alba*)

Habitat: open, sunny, disturbed sites, including pastures, old fields, meadows, roadsides, and fallow agricultural land

Broods: one or more generations possible; does not overwinter in the Midwest

Abundance: rare to occasional

Range: southern third of the region; rarer northward

Compare: Dainty Sulphur (pg. 317) is generally smaller and has a prominent black bar along trailing edge of the dorsal forewing plus black postmedian spots on the ventral forewing

Comments: A year-round resident of the Deep South, the Little Sulphur is a highly effective colonizer and common visitor each summer to much of the Midwest, where it establishes temporary breeding populations. Continuing climate warming has aided the northward range expansion and abundance of this butterfly in our region. It is typically more common from mid-summer into early fall. A small species, adults have a low, scurrying flight close to the ground.

Little Yellow
Pyrisitia lisa

Family/Subfamily: Whites and Sulphurs (Pieridae)/ Sulphurs (Coliadinae)

Wingspan: 1.0–1.6" (2.5–4.1 cm)

Above: bright yellow; forewing has a black tip, narrow black border, and often-faint cell spot; female is pale yellow to whitish with lighter black markings

Below: hindwing is yellow to whitish, with scattered dark markings and a pinkish spot on outer angle (often small or absent in males); wings often have pink fringes; seasonally variable; late-season individuals are darker yellow and more heavily patterned

Sexes: similar, although female is paler

Egg: white, spindle-shaped, laid singly on host leaves

Larva: green with thin cream side stripe

Larval Host Plants: primarily Partridge Pea (*Chamaecrista fasciculata*) and Sensitive Partridge Pea (*Chamaecrista nictitans*)

Habitat: open, sunny sites, including pastures, easements, old fields, meadows, roadsides, and forest margins

Broods: one to several generations; does not overwinter in the Midwest

Abundance: rare to common

Range: southern two-thirds of the region; sporadic and uncommon in more-northern locations

Compare: Orange Sulphur (pg. 325) has a rounded black forewing cell spot, uniform black wing borders, and a distinct central, pink-rimmed pearly cell spot on the ventral hindwing

Comments: Much debate centers on the origin of this butterfly's unique common name. One interpretation points to the narrow black forewing cell spot, which resembles a closed or partially closed eye. Others suggest that behavior is responsible. Individuals in the Deep South overwinter in reproductive diapause; they are highly sedentary during the winter but often become active on mild days to seek nectar. The Sleepy Orange is a seasonal colonist or sporadic vagrant to southern portions of our region. Like any other sulphur, it produces distinct seasonal forms that vary considerably in ventral hindwing color and pattern.

Sleepy Orange

Abaeis nicippe

Family/Subfamily: Whites and Sulphurs (Pieridae)/ Sulphurs (Coliadinae)

Wingspan: 1.3–2.0" (3.3–5.1 cm)

Above: bright orange with broad, irregular black wing borders; forewing has a small, elongated black cell spot

Below: hindwing is butter yellow with brown markings; seasonally variable; cool season individuals are tan to reddish brown with darker pattern elements

Sexes: similar, although female is larger and less vibrant with heavier ventral hindwing markings

Egg: white, spindle-shaped, laid singly on host leaves

Larva: green with thin cream side stripe

Larval Host Plants: various native, invasive, and ornamental sennas (*Senna* spp.), including Maryland Senna (*Senna marilandica*) and American Senna (*Senna hebecarpu*)

Habitat: open, sunny sites, including pastures, easements, old fields, meadows, roadsides, parks, and gardens

Broods: one to several generations; does not overwinter in the Midwest

Abundance: rare to occasional

Range: southern third of the region; sporadic, uncommon, or absent in more-northern locations

Compare: Clouded Sulphur (pg. 329) has a submarginal row of dark spots and double, pink-rimmed cell spot on ventral hindwing; inhabits open, disturbed sites and agricultural fields where clovers or vetches occur

Comments: Named for its prominent pink wing fringes, the Pink-Edged Sulphur is primarily a Canadian species that extends down into our region across the northern Great Lakes. It becomes increasingly encountered in the farther northern areas and can be locally common in sites that support extensive patches of its larval hosts. Adults have a meandering, weak flight and regularly visit a variety of low-growing flowers. Partially grown larvae overwinter and complete development the following spring.

Pink-Edged Sulphur

Colias interior

Family/Subfamily: Whites and Sulphurs (Pieridae)/ Sulphurs (Coliadinae)

Wingspan: 1.6–2.5" (4.0–6.35 cm)

Above: yellow with black wing borders and small black fore-wing cell spot; hindwing has a central faint orange spot; wing fringes are pink

Below: yellow with distinct pink fringes; hindwing with single pearly, pink rimmed cell spot

Sexes: similar, although female is paler and has reduced black wing borders only on the forewing

Egg: white, spindle-shaped, laid singly on host leaves

Larva: green with narrow red lateral stripe outlined in white

Larval Host Plants: blueberry (*Vaccinium* spp.)

Habitat: forest openings, bogs, barrens, woodland margins, and recently cleared or burned sites

Broods: one generation; young larvae overwinter

Abundance: rare to occasional; locally common

Range: northern tier of region

Compare: Clouded Sulphur (pg. 329) is lemon yellow and lacks orange scaling on the wings above; white-form female may not be readily separated in the field

Comments: Widespread and generally common across the US, the Orange Sulphur can be found in most open landscapes. Like the Clouded Sulphur, which it closely resembles, it is often most abundant in commercial Alfalfa or clover fields. The larvae are considered a minor agricultural pest. As a result of this strong host preference, it is frequently called the Alfalfa Butterfly. It is a prolific colonizer and readily populates new areas where native, naturalized, invasive, or cultivated leguminous plants abound. Adults have a rapid, somewhat erratic flight and scurry close to the ground over low vegetation.

Orange Sulphur
Colias eurytheme

Family/Subfamily: Whites and Sulphurs (Pieridae)/ Sulphurs (Coliadinae)

Wingspan: 1.6–2.75" (4.0–7.0 cm)

Above: bright yellow orange with black wing borders and a black forewing cell spot; hindwing has a central orange spot

Below: yellow with a row (often faint) of dark submarginal spots; pink wing fringes; hindwing has a central, red-rimmed silvery spot and adjacent, smaller satellite spot

Sexes: similar; female has less orange and wider black wing borders enclosing yellow spots; also has white form

Egg: white, spindle-shaped, laid singly on host leaves, turns orange

Larva: bluish green with longitudinal cream side stripe; marked with black below and often contains faint red dashes

Larval Host Plants: various pea plants (Fabaceae), including Alfalfa (*Medicago sativa*), Red Clover (*Trifolium pratense*), White Clover (*Trifolium repens*), and sweet clovers (*Melilotus* spp.) and vetches (*Vicia* spp.)

Habitat: open, sunny, disturbed sites, including Alfalfa fields, fallow agricultural land, old fields, meadows, roadsides, and yards

Broods: two or more generations; pupae overwinter

Abundance: occasional to abundant

Range: throughout

ventral

Compare: This is the only Sulphur in the region that has pointed forewings.

Comments: The Southern Dogface is named for its distinctive forewing pattern, which resembles (with some imagination) the head of a dog (poodle) in profile. This distinctive pattern is visible only in flight or when the wings are backlit. Adults feed and rest with their wings firmly closed. A resident of the Deep South, it is a migrant that temporarily colonizes or wanders into our region. As a result, its presence is highly sporadic and localized, and it varies considerably from year to year. Adults have a swift, rapid flight but frequently stop to drink nectar.

Southern Dogface
Zerene cesonia

Family/Subfamily: Whites and Sulphurs (Pieridae)/ Sulphurs (Coliadinae)

Wingspan: 1.9–2.6" (4.0–6.6 cm)

Above: yellow; forewing pointed with broad, black, highly scalloped margin that forms image of a dog's head in profile; has a single black cell spot and increased black basal scaling; hindwing has a narrow black margin

Below: hindwings seasonally variable; summer individuals are yellow with two small, central, pink-rimmed silver spots; late-season individuals have increased pink scaling

Sexes: similar, although black margins duller and less extensive in females

Egg: white, spindle-shaped, laid singly on host leaves

Larva: variable; plain green to green with white side striped, marked with orange dashes and transverse black and yellow stripes

Larval Host Plants: various pea plants (Fabaceae), including False Indigo (*Amorpha fruticosa*), Leadplant (*Amorpha canescens*), White Prairie Clover (*Dalea candida*), Purple Prairie Clover (*Dalea purpurea*), and Alfalfa (*Medicago sativa*)

Habitat: open, sunny sites, including prairies, pastures, old fields, meadows, roadsides, and woodland margins

Broods: one generation (or possibly more); does not overwinter in the Midwest

Abundance: rare to occasional; localized

Range: southern portions of the region

Compare: Orange Sulphur (pg. 325) has at least some orange scaling on the wings above; white-form female may not be readily separated in the field

Comments: Often seen flying alongside the similar-looking Orange Sulphur, it may be encountered in considerable numbers in commercial alfalfa or clover fields. Close observation is often needed to reliably separate the two species. It is sexually dimorphic and seasonally variable. Both yellow and white female forms are common. Cool-season individuals tend to be smaller and somewhat darker below than those of summer generations. Adults are fond of flowers and feed with their wings closed. Males often gather at damp ground.

Clouded Sulphur
Colias philodice

Family/Subfamily: White and Sulphurs (Pieridae)/ Sulphurs (Coliadinae)

Wingspan: 1.9–2.75" (4.8–7.0 cm)

Above: clear lemon yellow with bold, black wing borders; forewing with prominent black cell spot; hindwing with central orange spot

Below: yellow to greenish yellow; row (often faint or even absent) of dark submarginal spots; pink wing fringes; hindwing has central red-rimmed silvery spot and adjacent smaller satellite spot

Sexes: dissimilar; female is less vibrant with increased dusty black scaling and wider black wing borders enclosing yellow spots; also has white form

Egg: white, spindle-shaped, laid singly on host plant's leaves; turns orange

Larva: bluish-green with longitudinal cream side stripe, marked with black below and often containing faint red dashes

Larval Host Plants: various plants in the pea family (Fabaceae), including Alfalfa (*Medicago sativa*), Red Clover (*Trifolium pratense*), White Clover (*Trifolium repens*), sweet clovers (*Melilotus* spp.), and vetches (*Vicia* spp.)

Habitat: open, sunny, disturbed sites, including Alfalfa fields, fallow agricultural land, old fields, meadows, roadsides, and yards

Broods: two or more generations; pupae overwinter

Abundance: occasional to abundant

Range: throughout

Compare: Clouded Sulphur (pg. 329) and Orange Sulphur (pg. 325) are noticeably smaller; Southern Dogface (pg. 327) has pointed forewings

Comments: A sizable butterfly, the Cloudless Sulphur has a fast, powerful flight and is exceedingly fond of flowers. It rests and feeds with its wings firmly closed. Adults have a very long proboscis and can access nectar in many tubular blossoms unavailable to other butterflies. Abundant in the Deep South, it regularly colonizes southern portions of our region each year, being an increasingly rare vagrant the farther north you go. Unable to survive northern winters, adults migrate south each fall in large numbers to south Texas and peninsular Florida.

Cloudless Sulphur

Phoebis sennae

Family/Subfamily: White and Sulphurs (Pieridae)/
Sulphurs (Coliadinae)

Wingspan: 2.2–2.8" (5.6–7.1 cm)

Above: unmarked, bright lemon yellow; female has a black
dashed forewing border and black cell spot

Below: male is greenish yellow with very limited markings;
female is yellow with pinkish-brown markings and several
small, silvery spots in center of each wing; seasonally variable; late-season individuals are more heavily marked

Sexes: similar, although female is more heavily marked

Egg: white, spindle-shaped, laid singly on host leaves,
turns orange

Larva: green or yellow with a broad yellow side stripe and
numerous blue dots; may have blue transverse strips

Larval Host Plants: various pea plants (Fabaceae), includ-
ing Maryland Senna (*Senna marilandica*), Partridge Pea
(*Chamaecrista fasciculata*), and Sensitive Partridge Pea
(*Chamaecrista nictitans*)

Habitat: open, sunny sites, including prairies, pastures, old
fields, meadows, roadsides, parks, and gardens

Broods: one or more generations possible; does not overwinter
in Midwest

Abundance: rare to occasional

Range: southern portions of the region

Compare: Eastern Tiger Swallowtail (pg. 337) is larger, occurs in the southern two-thirds of the region, and has a broken submarginal spot band on the ventral forewing; females also have a dark form

Comments: This striking butterfly replaces the Eastern Tiger Swallowtail in northern portions of the region and is one of the best-known species in Canada. The two species are quite similar in appearance and are easily confused in areas where their ranges overlap. The Canadian Tiger Swallowtail is noticeably smaller than its southern counterpart, produces only one generation each year, and lacks a black female form. Somewhat melanotic female forms have been reported but are extremely rare. The adults are swift fliers and best observed at flowers. Males avidly congregate at mud puddles or other damp ground, sometimes in large numbers, to imbibe water and other nutrients.

Canadian Tiger Swallowtail

Papilio canadensis

Family/Subfamily: Swallowtails (Papilionidae)/
Swallowtails (Papilioninae)

Wingspan: 2.6–3.1" (6.6–7.9 cm)

Above: yellow with black forewing stripes and broad, black wing
margins; has a single row of yellow spots along outer edge of
each wing; hindwing has a noticeable eyespot near the single
prominent tail

Below: as above; abdomen is yellow with black stripes; hindwing
has increased blue scaling and single row of yellow to yellow-
orange, crescent-shaped spots along outer edge of each wing;
forewing has a continuous yellow submarginal band

Sexes: similar, although female is larger and has increased blue
hindwing scaling

Egg: green, round, laid singly on the upper surface of host
plant's leaves

Larva: green; enlarged thorax with two small false eyes; young
larvae are brown with a cream saddle

Larval Host Plants: various trees, including birch (*Betula* spp.),
Quaking Aspen (*Populus tremuloides*), ash (*Fraxinus* spp.),
Wild Cherry (*Prunus serotina*), and willow (*Salix* spp.)

Habitat: open deciduous and mixed forests; woodland margins;
and nearby open areas, including clearings, stream margins,
roadsides, yards, and gardens

Broods: one generation; pupae overwinter

Abundance: occasional to abundant

Range: throughout northern portions of the region

Compare: Eastern Tiger Swallowtail (pg. 337) has some orange scaling in the yellow marginal spots on the ventral hindwing; female has yellow and black form; and Two-Tailed Swallowtail (pg. 339) is larger and has two hindwing tails.

Comments: As its name implies, the Western Tiger Swallowtail is widespread and generally common across the American West, southern British Columbia, and northern Baja California. Its range extends eastward just into South Dakota and Nebraska where it is quickly replaced by the Eastern Tiger Swallowtail. Unlike its eastern relative, the species does not have a dark female form. Adults have a swift flight but are very fond of flowers and readily pause to nectar. Males frequently puddle at damp earth, animal dung, or urine.

Western Tiger Swallowtail

Papilio rutulus

Family/Subfamily: Swallowtails (Papilionidae)/
  Swallowtails (Papilioninae)

Wingspan: 2.9–4.0" (7.4–10.2 cm)

Above: yellow with black forewing stripes and broad black wing
  margins; single row of yellow spots along outer edge of each
  wing; hindwing has a black outer portion enclosing some
  blue scaling and a noticeable eyespot near a single tail

Below: as above, yellow with black stripes and black wing margins; abdomen is yellow with black stripes; hindwing has a
  single row of yellow spots along the outer edge of each wing

Sexes: similar; female has more blue scaling on dorsal hindwing

Egg: round, green, laid singly on upper surface of host leaves

Larva: green; enlarged thorax with two small false eyes; yellow
  and black transverse band behind thorax; young larvae are
  brown with a cream saddle

Larval Host Plants: cherry (*Prunus* spp.), ash (*Fraxinus* spp.), willow (*Salix* spp.), and cottonwood and aspen (*Populus* spp.)

Habitat: woodlands, stream corridors, parks, roadsides, gardens

Broods: one generation; pupae overwinter

Abundance: rare

Range: extreme western portions of the region

male

female

dark female

Compare: Canadian Tiger Swallowtail (pg. 333) occurs in more-northern areas of the region and has an unbroken submarginal spot band on the ventral forewing

Comments: Large and conspicuous, the Eastern Tiger Swallowtail is easily recognized by its bold black stripes and bright-yellow wings. Adults have a strong, swift flight and often soar high in the treetops. Although common in and near deciduous woodlands, it is equally at home in urban parks and forested neighborhoods, where it is a frequent garden visitor. Unlike many other swallowtails, the adults tend not to flutter their wings continuously as they feed at flowers. They instead rest with their wings outstretched, making them quite visible even from a distance. Dark-form females mimic the toxic Pipevine Swallowtail (pg. 41) to gain protection from primarily avian predators. Males often congregate at moist earth, urine, or animal dung.

Eastern Tiger Swallowtail
Papilio gluacus

Family/Subfamily: Swallowtails (Papilionidae)/
  Swallowtails (Papilioninae)

Wingspan: 3.5–5.0" (8.9–12.7 cm)

Above: yellow with black forewing stripes and broad, black wing
  margins; has a single row of yellow spots along outer edge of
  each wing; hindwing has a noticeable eyespot near the single
  prominent tail

Below: as above; abdomen is yellow with black stripes; has a
  single row of yellow to yellow-orange spots along outer edge
  of each wing

Sexes: dissimilar; males are always yellow, but females have
  both a yellow and a dark (black) form

Egg: green, round, laid singly on the upper surface of
  host leaves

Larva: green; enlarged thorax with two small false eyes; young
  larvae are brown with a cream saddle

Larval Host Plants: various trees, including Wild Cherry (*Prunus
  serotina*), Chokecherry (*Prunus virginiana*), ash (*Fraxinus*
  spp.), and Tulip Tree (*Liriodendron tulipifera*)

Habitat: deciduous forests and nearby open areas, including
  gardens, parks, fields, and roadsides

Broods: two or more generations; pupae overwinter

Abundance: occasional to very common

Range: mostly throughout; absent from northern portions;
  uncommon or absent from extreme western portions

Compare: Western Tiger Swallowtail (pg. 335) and Eastern Tiger Swallowtail (pg. 337) both have only one hindwing tail and less pointed forewing tips

Comments: A spectacular butterfly in size and appearance, the Two-Tailed Swallowtail is widespread across much of the West from western North Dakota to Texas and west to California. Aptly named, each of its hindwings bear two distinct tails. Powerful fliers, the adults readily visit available blooms, feeding with the boldly patterned wings outstretched. The plump green larvae spin a silken pad and rest on the upper surface of host leaves when not actively feeding.

Two-Tailed Swallowtail

Papilio multicuadata

Family/Subfamily: Swallowtails (Papilionidae)/
Swallowtails (Papilioninae)

Wingspan: 3.5–5.75" (8.8–14.7 cm)

Above: forewing apex is somewhat pointed; yellow with black
forewing stripes and broad black wing margins; single row
of yellow spots along outer edge of each wing; hindwing has
black outer portion enclosing blue scaling and a noticeable
eyespot near two prominent tails

Below: as above, yellow with black stripes and black wing margins; abdomen is yellow with black stripes; hindwing has a
row of yellow to yellow-orange spots on outer edge

Sexes: similar; female has more blue scaling on dorsal hindwing

Egg: green, round, laid singly on the upper surface of host
plant's leaves

Larva: green; enlarged thorax with two small false eyes; yellow-
and-black transverse band behind thorax; young larvae are
brown with cream saddle

Larval Host Plants: cherry (*Prunus* spp.) and ash (*Fraxinus* spp.)

Habitat: open woodlands, stream corridors, parks, roadsides,
and gardens

Broods: one generation; pupae overwinter

Abundance: rare to occasional

Range: extreme western portions of the region

MOTHS

When you're observing butterflies, there's a good chance you'll come across moths. Moths, like butterflies, belong to the order Lepidoptera, and they are well known for primarily being active at night and for their often-drab, cryptic coloration. Nonetheless, there are an estimated 11,000 (or more) moth species in the US and more than 150,000 worldwide, and as a group they deserve a closer look.

As a whole, moths are incredibly diverse, much more so than butterflies, and many upend the common stereotypes many folks have about them. Some, such as certain sphinx moths (page 353 and 383), are fast-flying, highly visible, and active during the day, when they may be mistaken for hummingbirds. Others, such as the stunning Luna Moth or Polyphemus Moth, are large, brightly colored, and attracted to lights at night. Even the drab, hard-to-identify species can be staggeringly beautiful.

The following accounts are a general introduction to a handful of the more commonly spotted moths in our region. As in the butterflies section, the moths are organized first by their primary **color** and then by **size.**

Compare: unique

Comments: Named for the total number of distinctive spots on its wings, the Eight-Spotted Forester is an energetic and charismatic species. Active by day, the adults readily visit flowers in search of nectar and are often mistaken for small butterflies. They have a quick, darting flight and energetically flit from one blossom to another.

Eight-Spotted Forester
Alypia octomaculata

Family/Subfamily: Cutworm Moths and Allies (Noctuidae)/ Forester Moths (Agaristinae)

Wingspan: 1.0–1.5" (2.5–3.8 cm)

Above: wings are black (often with bluish cast) and somewhat rounded; forewing has two large, yellow spots; hindwing has two large white spots; body black; thorax has yellow shoulders; front and middle legs have brilliant orange hair tufts; long, slender antennae

Below: as above

Sexes: similar

Egg: oval, green, laid on host

Larva: white with transverse black line and spots; wider transverse orange bands, and scattered long hairs; head is orange with black spots

Larval Host Plants: Virginia Creeper (*Parthenocissus quinquefolia*) and grape (*Vitis* spp.)

Habitat: forest openings, margins, and adjacent open areas

Broods: one to two generations; pupae overwinter

Abundance: occasional to common

Range: generally throughout, although less common in far northern portions

Compare: unique

Comments: The Virginia Ctenucha is a distinctive and superficially drab day-flying moth. Upon closer inspection, though, it displays a brilliant metallic blue body and is one of several such species that mimic wasps to gain protection from predators. The adults have a somewhat weak, fluttering flight and frequently land on vegetation. They feed on nectar and may be quite commonly encountered on various flowers, particularly in meadows and open fields. Its unusual genus name, Ctenucha, means "has a comb" in Greek and refers to the male's distinctive antennae. The hairy larvae overwinter in leaf litter or among vegetation and construct a loose cocoon the following spring.

Virginia Ctenucha
Ctenucha virginica

Family/Subfamily: Underwing, Tiger, Tussock, and Allied Moths (Erebidae)/Tiger Moths (Arctiinae)

Wingspan: 1.5–2.0" (3.8–5.1 cm)

Above: rounded, drab black wings; metallic blue body and orange head; long antennae

Below: as above

Sexes: similar, although males have noticeably feathery antennae

Egg: oval, yellow, laid in clusters on host leaves

Larva: black body with cream lateral stripe; covered in dense tufts of black and cream and/or yellow hairs

Larval Host Plants: various grasses and some sedges

Habitat: forest openings, meadows, prairie, old fields

Broods: one to two generations; larvae overwinter

Abundance: occasional to common

Range: northeastern portion of the region

Virgin Tiger Moth
Grammia virgo

Family/Subfamily: Underwing, Tiger, Tussock, and Allied Moths (Erebidae)/Tiger Moths (Arctiinae)

Wingspan: 2.0–2.25" (5.1–5.7 cm)

Habitat: woodlands and margins, parks, and adjacent open areas; occasional to common

Range: eastern two-thirds of the region

Sexes: similar

Larva: densely hairy; hairs are black dorsally and tawny orange along the sides

Above: forewing is black with crossing cream lines and borders; hindwing is pinkish with large black spots; thorax is black with cream lines; abdomen is pink with black spots

Below: as above but paler

Compare: unique

Comments: This boldly patterned moth is widespread across the Northeast and portions of the Midwest. The adults are nocturnal and are frequently attracted to artificial lights. The sizable, hairy larvae have a typical woolly bear appearance.

Eastern Buckmoth

Hemileuca maia

Family/Subfamily: Emperor, Royal, Moon, and Giant Silk Moths (Saturniidae)/Buck and Io Moths (Hemileucinae)

Wingspan: 2.0–3.0" (5.1–7.6 cm)

Habitat: oak woodlands, barrens, and parks

Range: primarily eastern portions; uncommon to occasional

Sexes: similar, although the tip of the abdomen is red in males

Larva: variable; black with numerous tiny white dots and several rows of venomous, black branched spines; dorsal two rows often lighter colored; larvae pupate in leaf litter or soil

Above: wings are black with a broad white median band; each wing has a narrow, dark cell spot; hairy black body in females; male body is black with a red tip to the abdomen

Below: as above

Compare: unique

Comments: Found in mid-to-late fall, adults are active during the day. Females lay eggs in rings around host twigs. Larvae feed exclusively on oak (*Quercus* spp.) and are gregarious when young.

female

male

Compare: Tuliptree Silkmoth (pg. 363) females are very similar but are typically more yellow brown or orange brown dorsally

Comments: Unlike most other giant silk moths, this lovely species is strikingly dimorphic and appears radically different. Males are primarily black, fly during the day, and mimic the toxic Pipevine Swallowtail. By contrast, females are rosy colored, nocturnal, and periodically attracted to artificial lights. Mating takes place in late afternoon, when females begin releasing pheromones. The volatile chemicals can travel long distances, and males are able to pick up the scent from miles away. The showy larvae feed gregariously when young, becoming more solitary with age. They spin an elongated, pendulous silken cocoon that attaches to a host branch. They are easily spotted in winter on leafless trees.

Promethea Silkmoth

Callosamia promethea

Family/Subfamily: Emperor, Royal, Moon, and Giant Silk Moths (Saturniidae)/Giant Silk Moths (Saturniinae)

Wingspan: 2.8–3.7" (7.1–9.4 cm)

Above: sexually dimorphic; male is black with light-brown borders and a prominent eyespot on the forewing apex; female is two-toned pinkish brown with darker wing bases, tan borders, and a prominent eyespot on the forewing apex; each wing has a narrow, irregular, light cell spot in the center

Below: similar to above but lighter and with extensive pinkish scaling on the outer half of the hindwing in both sexes

Sexes: dissimilar; males are black and females are pinkish brown

Egg: oval, cream, laid in small clusters on host leaves

Larva: plump, greenish white with rows of pale, blue–rimmed black spots, four black-based red knobs on the thorax, and one black-based yellow knob on the rear

Larval Host Plants: numerous trees and shrubs, including ash (*Fraxinus* spp.), cherry and plum (*Prunus* spp.), Spicebush (*Lindera benzoin*), Sassafras (*Sassafras albidum*), and Common Lilac (*Syringa vulgaris*)

Habitat: deciduous forests, parks, and yards

Broods: one generation; pupae overwinter

Abundance: occasional to common

Range: eastern half of the region; rare or absent westward

Compare: unique

Comments: The delicate-looking adults are nocturnal and frequently attracted to artificial lights. The variably colored larvae are quite conspicuous and more commonly encountered. The dense hairs conceal the body and help protect it from predators. While the hairs do not sting, some people, especially those with sensitive skin, may still occasionally experience some irritation when handling the larvae.

Banded Tussock Moth

Halysidota tessellaris

Family/Subfamily: Underwing, Tiger, Tussock, and Allied Moths (Erebidae)/Tiger Moths (Arctiinae)

Wingspan: 1.5–1.75" (3.8–4.4 cm)

Above: elongated forewings; wings are pale yellow to cream yellow and almost translucent; forewing has somewhat darker bands edged in fine dark lines; hindwing is unmarked

Below: as above

Sexes: similar

Egg: pale green, laid in clusters on underside of host leaves

Larva: densely hairy; variable in color; light gray, yellow, or orange with darker dorsal stripe and elongated black-and-white hair tufts on both ends

Larval Host Plants: various trees and shrubs, including oak, ash, hickory, willow, birch, elm, and poplar

Habitat: woodlands and margins, parks, and adjacent open areas

Broods: one to two generations; pupae overwinter in silken cocoons

Abundance: occasional to abundant

Range: throughout, although less common in far western areas

Compare: Snowberry Clearwing (pg. 383) is very similar but has black legs and a black line that runs across the eye and down the side of the thorax

Comments: These charismatic and entertaining day-flying moths are frequent garden visitors. Behaving like a small humming-bird, they maneuver from blossom to blossom, pausing briefly in front of each flower to uncurl their long proboscis and sip sugary nectar. The rapid motion of their mostly transparent wings even causes an audible buzzing noise when the insects are nearby. Their bumblebee-like appearance presumably provides protection from would-be predators.

Hummingbird Clearwing

Hemaris thysbe

Family/Subfamily: Sphinx Moths (Sphingidae)/Macroglossine Sphinx Moths (Macroglossinae)

Wingspan: 1.5–2.25" (3.8–5.7 cm)

Above: elongated wings; stout, hairy body; thorax and first segments of abdomen are olive to golden; posterior portions are burgundy to blackish; wings are transparent with burgundy to reddish-brown borders; legs are light in color

Below: as above but slightly paler

Sexes: similar

Egg: oval, light green, laid singly on host leaves

Larva: light green to yellow green with tiny yellow spots; a small red side spot on each abdominal segment; and a short, curved horn off the rear

Larval Host Plants: various plants, including honeysuckle (*Lonicera* spp.), cherry (*Prunus* spp.), hawthorn (*Crataegus* spp.), and snowberry (*Symphoricarpos* spp.)

Habitat: forest margins, shrubby areas, meadows, old fields, parks, gardens, and urban areas

Broods: one to two generations; pupae overwinter

Abundance: occasional to common

Range: primarily eastern half of the region; uncommon or absent in extreme western portions

Compare: unique

Comments: Found across the US and southern Canada, this delightful moth is often encountered at artificial lights. Nonetheless, it is the larva that gets all the attention. Also called the Banded Woolly Bear, it is one of our most beloved and well-known caterpillars. Often spotted in late summer or fall when wandering quickly along the ground or crossing roads to find a protected location in which to overwinter. While it is commonly believed that the width of the colored bands on the larvae predict the severity of the upcoming winter, their color is actually determined by other factors, including age. To protect themselves against frigid winter temperatures, the larvae also produce increased blood levels of glycerol, which acts as a natural antifreeze.

Isabella Tiger Moth
Pyrrharctia Isabella

Family/Subfamily: Underwing, Tiger, Tussock, and Allied Moths (Erebidae)/Tiger Moths (Arctiinae)

Wingspan: 1.75–2.5" (4.4–6.4 cm)

Above: forewing is pale orange yellow; apex is somewhat pointed; hindwing is pale yellow to cream in males; pinkish orange in females; both wings have scattered faint dark spots

Below: as above

Sexes: similar, although males have paler hindwings

Egg: oval, cream, laid in clusters on host leaves

Larva: densely hairy; reddish orange with black on each end

Larval Host Plants: a wide variety of herbaceous and woody plants, including numerous weedy species such as plantain (*Plantago* spp.), goldenrod (*Solidago* spp.), and sweetclover (*Melilotus* spp.)

Habitat: meadows, prairie, old fields, forest margins, fallow agricultural lands, roadsides, and yards

Broods: one to two generations; larvae overwinter

Abundance: occasional to common

Range: throughout

Compare: unique

Comments: Occurring throughout the US and southern Canada, the White-Lined Sphinx is one of our most commonly encountered moths. The sizable, stout-bodied adults are typically nocturnal and are most often encountered during the low-light periods of dawn and dusk. Nonetheless, they may also occasionally be spotted during the day. Behaving like hummingbirds and often mistaken for them, the adults navigate from flower to flower, acquiring nectar with their long proboscis, pausing only briefly before moving on to the next bloom. The horned larvae vary considerably and may be mostly green or more heavily patterned.

White-Lined Sphinx

Hyles lineata

Family/Subfamily: Sphinx Moths (Sphingidae)/Macroglossine Sphinx Moths (Macroglossinae)

Wingspan: 2.2–3.5" (5.6–8.9 cm)

Above: elongated wings and body; forewing is brown with a broad, pale central stripe, white veins, and a pale outer border; hindwing is pink with dark-brown borders; dark-brown thorax striped in white; light-brown abdomen marked on the back with black-and-white spots

Below: pale, drab brown; each wing has a pale, dark brown-bordered central band

Sexes: similar

Egg: oval, light green, laid on host leaves

Larva: highly variable; bright green with black longitudinal stripes, black-outlined yellow-and-pink spots on each segment, and a curved orange (or black-lipped orange) horn off the rear

Larval Host Plants: a wide variety of plants, including evening primrose (*Oenothera* spp.) and four o'clock (*Mirabilis* spp.)

Habitat: forest openings and margins, shrubby areas, meadows, old fields, parks, gardens, and urban areas

Broods: two generations; pupae overwinter

Abundance: occasional to common

Range: throughout

Compare: unique

Comments: A showy species, the Blinded Sphinx is widespread and generally common across much of the US and southern Canada. Adults are nocturnal and are attracted to artificial lights. The species' odd common name comes from the lack of a hindwing eyespot without a central black "pupil." Adults rest with their cryptically patterned forewings lowered covering the spotted and more colorful hindwings, which are quickly revealed if disturbed.

Blinded Sphinx

Paonias excaecata

Family/Subfamily: Sphinx Moths (Sphingidae)/
Sphinx Moths (Sphinginae)

Wingspan: 2.3–3.7" (5.8–9.4 cm)

Above: elongated wings; forewing is mottled with tan, pink, and brown; outer margins are noticeably scalloped; hindwing is pink basally with a large, central, blue-centered black eyespot; outer hindwing margin is pale; has a stout, elongated body

Below: forewing is pink with a mottled brown outer margin; hindwing is mottled tan, pink, cream, and brown

Sexes: similar

Egg: pale green, laid singly on host leaves

Larva: bright green with tiny yellow spots; each abdominal segment has an oblique yellow dash and red spot; curved horn off the rear

Larval Host Plants: various trees, including cherry, birch, willow, poplar, and oak

Habitat: woodlands and margins, yards, and parks

Broods: one to two generations; pupae overwinter in soil

Abundance: occasional to common

Range: throughout, although less common in far western areas

Compare: unique

Comments: Aptly named, underwing moths are named for their boldly colored hindwings, which are typically obscured by the bark-like patterned forewings when at rest. Often spotted on tree trunks or vegetation, these moths immediately flash the colorfully banded hindwings if startled and may fly off quickly with additional disturbance. This behavior acts to potentially startle a would-be predator. The large adults are nocturnal and active in late summer into fall. They feed on tree sap and may be drawn in by sugary or fermented baits.

Penitent Underwing

Catocala piatrix

Family/Subfamily: Erebid Moths (Erebidae)/
Erebine Moths (Erebinae)

Wingspan: 2.6–3.1" (6.6–8.0 cm)

Above: forewing has a gray-brown, mottled, bark-like pattern
with light and dark bands and black lines; hindwing is
banded with light orange and black; margin is pale

Below: pale, forewing and hindwing have darker bands

Sexes: similar

Egg: small grayish eggs, laid in crevices of bark on host trees

Larva: dull gray with a somewhat-blue cast; elongated and
tapering at both ends

Larval Host Plants:

Habitat: woodlands and margins, parks, and forested yards

Broods: one generation; eggs overwinter

Abundance: uncommon to occasional

Range: southeastern half of the region

Compare: Promethea Silkmoth (pg. 349) females are very similar but are typically more pinkish or rosy dorsally and lack any yellow or orange-brown color; males are generally mostly black, are not noticeably two-toned, and lack the irregular cell spots on each wing

Comments: As its name suggests, this showy species is a specialist of Tuliptrees. Unlike the similar-looking Promethea Silkmoth, males resemble a dark-brown version of the female and both sexes are active at night. The species is widespread throughout much of the eastern US, from the Florida panhandle to southern Michigan, but it is particularly common across the Appalachian region. The larvae feed gregariously when young, becoming more solitary with age. They spin an elongated, pendulous, and often leaf-wrapped silken cocoon that attaches to a host branch.

Tuliptree Silkmoth

Callosamia angulifera

Family/Subfamily: Emperor, Royal, Moon, and Giant Silk Moths (Saturniidae)/Giant Silk Moths (Saturniinae)

Wingspan: 3.0–4.3" (7.6–10.9 cm)

Above: sexually dimorphic; male is two-toned with darker wing bases, an irregular median line, and light borders; female is typically two-toned with orange-brown to yellow-brown (and some pink), with darker wing bases and light borders; both sexes have a prominent eyespot on the forewing apex and narrow, irregular, light cell spots in the center of each wing

Below: similar to above but lighter and with extensive lighter scaling on the outer half of the hindwing in both sexes

Sexes: dissimilar; males are black and females are orange brown to yellow brown

Egg: oval, cream, laid in small clusters on host leaves

Larva: plump, greenish white with rows of small black spots, four black-based red knobs on the thorax, and black-based one yellow knob on the rear; knobs somewhat less prominent than in the Promethea Silkmoth

Larval Host Plants: Tuliptree (*Liriodendron tulipifera*)

Habitat: deciduous forests, parks, and yards

Broods: one to two generations; pupae overwinter

Abundance: occasional

Range: southeastern portion of the region

Compare: Carolina Sphinx (pg. 371) is very similar but has six yellow-orange spots on the abdomen; larva has white oblique dashes—not V-shaped markings—on the abdominal segments and a reddish horn off the rear

Comments: The large, robust, and generally drab adults are crepuscular. They have very long proboscises and feed like hummingbirds at tubular flowers. Despite this behavior, most people are much more familiar with the Five-Spotted Hawkmoth larvae. Also called Tomato Hornworms, the small, hot dog–sized larvae are commonly spotted in gardens, where they can be pests of various vegetables. When mature, the larvae crawl off the host and pupate in the soil.

Five-Spotted Hawkmoth

Manduca quinquemaculata

Family/Subfamily: Sphinx Moths (Sphingidae)/
Sphinx Moths (Sphinginae)

Wingspan: 3.5–5.2" (8.9–13.2 cm)

Above: elongated wings; forewing is a mottled gray, cream, and
brown in a bark-like pattern; hindwing is light gray with wavy
dark-gray to black lines and darker margin; elongated, stout
gray body has five black-outlined yellow-orange spots

Below: as above but paler and more uniform light gray

Sexes: similar

Egg: oval, light green, laid singly on host leaves

Larva: large, green with white V-shaped marks on each abdominal segment and a curved black horn off the rear

Larval Host Plants: various plants in the nightshade family
(Solanaceae), including peppers, eggplants, potatoes,
and tomatoes

Habitat: agricultural fields, gardens, and urban areas

Broods: two or more generations; pupae overwinter

Abundance: occasional to common

Range: mostly throughout; uncommon or absent in extreme
northern portions

Compare: unique

Comments: Widespread across the US and southern Canada, this distinctive species is one of our largest moths. When at rest, the Polyphemus Moth's brown wings provide useful camouflage. If disturbed, however, it opens and often flaps its wings to expose the large and realistic hindwing eyespots. This defensive behavior serves to potentially startle a predator or deflect its attack away from the insect's vulnerable body. The adults are active at night and readily attracted to artificial lights. Larvae construct a thick, pale, silken cocoon about the size of a hen's egg. They are typically attached to a twig or branch and hang downward, often making them easy to spot on leafless trees in winter.

Polyphemus Moth

Antheraea Polyphemus

Family/Subfamily: Emperor, Royal, Moon, and Giant Silk Moths (Saturniidae)/Giant Silk Moths (Saturniinae)

Wingspan: 4.0–5.8" (10.0–14.7 cm)

Above: variable; tan, grayish-brown to reddish-brown wings; forewing has a single small, yellow-rimmed eyespot in the center; hindwing has a large, prominent oval eyespot outlined in yellow, blue, and black; has a hairy body and ferny antennae, most prominent in males

Below: wings are marked with brown, gray, and pink with a cryptic dead-leaf-like pattern

Sexes: similar, although males have smaller bodies and large, ferny antennae

Egg: oval, somewhat flattened, cream, ringed with brown

Larva: plump; bright green with brown head, oblique lateral yellow lines on each abdominal segment, and red spots

Larval Host Plants: many different broadleaf trees and shrubs, including oak (*Quercus* spp.), birch (*Betula* spp.), maple (*Acer* spp.), dogwood (*Cornus* spp.), willow (*Salix* spp.), and elm (*Ulmus* spp.)

Habitat: deciduous forests, wetlands, parks, and yards

Broods: one to two generations; cocoons overwinter

Abundance: occasional to common

Range: throughout

Compare: unique

Comments: Sizable and boldly patterned, the Cecropia Moth
is one of our most spectacular large moths. As it is found a
variety of different habitats, including suburban and urban
settings, it may also be one of the most frequently encountered. The adults are nocturnal and occasionally attracted
to artificial lights. Its distinctive larvae, though, may even
be more familiar. Often exceeding four inches in length, the
chubby larvae are adorned with colorful, knobby projections
called tubercles. When fully grown, the larvae construct a
large, brown, and somewhat papery silken cocoon that is
typically attached lengthwise to a branch.

Cecropia Moth
Hyalophora cecropia

Family/Subfamily: Emperor, Royal, Moon, and Giant Silk Moths (Saturniidae)/Giant Silk Moths (Saturniinae)

Wingspan: 4.5–6.0" (11.4–15.2 cm)

Above: wings are dark gray brown with scattered white scales and tan margin; forewing has a red-and-white central band and a prominent dark eyespot near the apex; hindwing has broad red-and-white postmedian band; all wings have a central crescent-shaped cell spot; has a hairy red-and-white body

Below: as above but slightly lighter

Sexes: similar, although females are larger and have less-pronounced, ferny antennae

Egg: oval, cream, with reddish-brown mottling; laid on host plant's leaves

Larva: plump, bluish green with knobby blue, yellow, and reddish-orange tubercles, each with short, black spines; Blue tubercles occur along the sides, and there are yellow ones along the top of the abdominal segments, and four reddish-orange ones on the top of the thorax

Larval Host Plants: a wide variety of trees and shrubs in many families, including maple (*Acer* spp.), willow (*Salix* spp.), birch (*Betula* spp.), serviceberry (*Amelanchier* spp.), cherry (*Prunus* spp.), and apple (*Malus* spp.)

Habitat: deciduous forests, wetlands, parks, and yards

Broods: one to two generations; pupae overwinter

Abundance: occasional to common

Range: nearly throughout; less common or absent in far western portions of the region

Compare: Five-Spotted Hawkmoth (pg. 365) has only five yellow-orange spots on the abdomen; the larva has v-shaped markings on side of the body and a black rear horn

Comments: Adult Carolina Sphinx Moths are crepuscular. They navigate the low-light environment, flying quickly but pausing to feed at tubular blooms like a hummingbird. The more frequently encountered larvae are also called Tobacco Hornworms. Plump and large at maturity, they feed on various garden vegetables, including tomato plants. Possessing voracious appetites, the munching larvae can quickly devour or even defoliate plants. The mature larvae do not spin cocoons but instead pupate in the soil.

Carolina Sphinx

Manduca sexta

Family/Subfamily: Sphinx Moths (Sphingidae)/
Sphinx Moths (Sphinginae)

Wingspan: 3.5–5.0" (8.9–12.7 cm)

Above: elongated forewing is mottled gray, cream, and brown;
bark-like pattern; hindwing is light gray with wavy dark-gray
to black lines; darker margin; gray body has six black-outlined
yellow-orange spots

Below: as above but paler and more uniform light gray

Sexes: similar

Egg: small, green, laid singly on host leaves

Larva: large, green with white oblique dashes on each abdominal segment, and a curved reddish horn off the rear

Larval Host Plants: various plants in the nightshade family
(Solanaceae), including tomato, potato, tobacco, pepper
and eggplant

Habitat: agricultural fields, gardens, and urban areas

Broods: two generations, pupae overwinter in the soil

Abundance: occasional to common

Range: southern half of region; uncommon or absent in extreme
northern parts; occasional to common

Compare: unique

Comments: Hauntingly beautiful and considered by many to be among our most attractive insects, the Luna Moth is named for the Roman moon goddess. The nocturnal adults are strong fliers and readily attracted to artificial lights. They tend to be most common in more-forested areas and tend not to adapt well to heavy urbanization. More than for show, their long hindwing tails spin during flight, causing an acoustic signal that helps divert bat attacks. When done feeding, the larva constructs a papery brown, often leaf-wrapped cocoon on the ground among other leaf litter.

Luna Moth
Actias luna

Family/Subfamily: Emperor, Royal, Moon, and Giant Silk Moths (Saturniidae)/Giant Silk Moths (Saturniinae)

Wingspan: 3.0–4.0" (7.5–10.0 cm)

Above: light green; forewing has an oval cell-end eyespot; hindwing has a central eyespot and a long, twisted tail; wing margins are pink in early-season adults; has hairy white body; ferny antennae are most prominent in males

Below: as above only slightly paler

Sexes: similar, although males have smaller bodies and large, ferny antennae

Egg: oval, cream, mottled with brown

Larva: plump; bright green with a pale yellow lateral stripe, transverse pale-yellow stripes along the back of most segments, and pink spots

Larval Host Plants: numerous broadleaf trees, including birch (*Betula* spp.), walnut (*Juglans* spp.), hickory (*Carya* spp.), and Sweetgum (*Liquidambar styraciflua*)

Habitat: deciduous forests

Broods: one to two generations; cocoons overwinter

Abundance: occasional to common

Range: eastern two-thirds of the region; rare or absent westward

Compare: unique

Comments: Large and extremely showy, this is without a doubt one of our most spectacular sphinx moths. Adults most often encountered at dusk or dawn as they feed at flowers and are also attracted to artificial lights at night. At rest, their mossy green and brown coloration provides superb camouflage. The adult moths may be overshadowed by their chubby, and highly charismatic larvae, which have several color forms. At maturity, they pupate in shallow underground chambers in the soil.

Pandorus Sphinx

Eumorpha pandorus

Family/Subfamily: Sphinx Moths (Sphingidae)/Macroglossine Sphinx Moths (Macroglossinae

Wingspan: 3.0–4.5" (7.6–11.4 cm)

Above: elongated wings; wings are olive green with light-brown and pink streaks and some darker green patches; stout, elongated body

Below: uniform pale olive-green, with lighter borders along the outer margin

Sexes: similar

Egg: round, translucent and green; laid singly on host leaves

Larva: variable; green, reddish brown to chocolate with prominent black-centered, white, circular eyespots on each abdominal segment

Larval Host Plants: grape (*Vitis* spp.) and Virginia creeper (*Parthenocissus quinquefolia*)

Habitat: forest edges and openings, stream corridors, gardens, yards, parks, and urban areas

Broods: one to two generations; pupae overwinter in the soil

Abundance: occasional to common

Range: eastern two-thirds of the region; uncommon or absent westward and in extreme northern portions

Compare: unique

Comments: Without a doubt, the Regal Moth is one of most spectacular moths in North America, impressive in both size and sheer beauty. Although it is widespread across the Southeast, many people seldom encounter the nocturnal adults and are more familiar with the species' iconic larva. Aptly named the Hickory Horned Devil, it boasts a truly alarming appearance and reaches about the size of a bratwurst at maturity. Larvae do not spin cocoons but pupate underground instead. As a result, they tend to be encountered wandering on the ground as they search for a suitable location to pupate.

Regal Moth
Citheronia regalis

Family/Subfamily: Emperor, Royal, Moon, and Giant Silk Moths (Saturniidae)/Royal Moths (Ceratocampinae)

Wingspan: 3.75–6.0" (9.5–15.2 cm)

Above: forewing is grayish to gray green with orange veins and cream-yellow spots; hindwing is orange with yellow along the leading and anal margins and often some gray postmedian spots or streaks; has a hairy orange and yellow body

Below: forewing as above but paler; hindwing is creamy yellow basally with orange veins and gray scaling toward outer margin

Sexes: similar, although females are often much larger

Egg: oval, cream, laid on host leaves

Larva: large, bluish green with an orange head and wide, oblique cream dashes on each abdominal segment, outlined by black along the top; thorax bears long, curved, black-tipped orange-red horns

Larval Host Plants: broadleaf trees, including walnut (*Juglans* spp.), hickory (*Carya* spp.), Common Persimmon (*Diospyros virginiana*), and Sweetgum (*Liquidambar styraciflua*)

Habitat: deciduous forests

Broods: one generation; pupae overwinter

Abundance: uncommon to occasional

Range: southeastern portions of the region

Compare: unique

Comments: This lovely, ghostly white moth is widespread and
generally common across much of the US and southern
Canada. Adults are nocturnal and regularly attracted to
artificial lights. When disturbed, the adult mot curls its
abdomen and plays dead, displaying the bright colors on
its abdomen. The large, hairy larvae are commonly encountered on many plants and often referred to as the Yellow
Woolly Bear. They are gregarious when young, becoming
solitary with age.

Virginian Tiger Moth
Spilosoma virginica

Family/Subfamily: Underwing, Tiger, Tussock, and Allied Moths (Erebidae)/Tiger Moths (Arctiinae)

Wingspan: 1.25–2.0" (3.2–5.1 cm)

Above: wings are pure white, often marked with a few scattered black spots; hairy white body; abdomen marked with broad yellow-orange bands bordered on each side by black spots

Below: as above

Sexes: similar

Egg: round, yellow, laid in clusters on the underside of host leaves

Larva: variable in color; body with dense cream-yellow to orange to reddish-brown hairs

Larval Host Plants: generalist herbivores feeding on many different herbaceous and woody plants

Habitat: woodlands and margins, parks, yards, and gardens

Broods: two generations; larvae overwinter

Abundance: occasional to common

Range: throughout

Compare: unique

Comments: Although relatively small, the Rosy Maple Moth is one of our showiest species. Gaudily colored in pink, the flashy adults are nocturnal and readily attracted to artificial lights. Like other giant silk moths, the adults have vestigial mouthparts and do not feed, living instead off fat reserves. As a result, they have relatively short adult life spans. The distinctive larvae feed gregariously when young, becoming solitary with age. They can occasionally become pests, causing aesthetic damage to maple trees. When mature, the larvae retreat and pupate in the ground.

Rosy Maple Moth
Dryocampa rubicunda

Family/Subfamily: Emperor, Royal, Moon, and Giant Silk Moths (Saturniidae)/Royal Moths (Ceratocampinae)

Wingspan: 1.25–2.0" (3.2–5.1 cm)

Above: variable; forewing is bright pink with a broad cream-to-yellow median band becoming broader toward the leading margin; hindwing is cream to yellow with a broad, often-faint pink border; fuzzy yellow body and pink legs

Below: as above but often somewhat lighter

Sexes: similar

Egg: oval, yellow, laid in clusters on host leaves

Larva: yellow green with longitudinal rows of dark-green, cream, or black stripes; several rows of short black spines; two long horns off the thorax; and a reddish head

Larval Host Plants: various maples (*Acer* spp.)

Habitat: deciduous forests, parks, yards, and urban areas

Broods: one to two generations; pupae overwinter

Abundance: occasional to common

Range: eastern half of the region; rare or absent westward

Compare: Hummingbird Clearwing (pg. 353) is very similar but has light legs and lacks a black line that runs across the eye and down the side of the thorax

Comments: This charismatic species is widespread throughout the eastern US and southern Canada. Somewhat variable, it is often confused with the similar-looking Hummingbird Clearwing, with which it geographically overlaps. Like its close relative, the Snowberry Clearwing is active by day. It readily scurries around from flower to flower like a bee or butterfly, hovering briefly in front of each bloom to acquire nectar. The distinctive larvae have both green and brown forms and bear a protruding horn off the rear.

Snowberry Clearwing

Hemaris diffinis

Family/Subfamily: Sphinx Moths (Sphingidae)/Macroglossine Sphinx Moths (Macroglossinae)

Wingspan: 1.3–2.0" (3.3–5.1 cm)

Above: color variable; elongated wings; stout, hairy body; thorax and first segments of the abdomen are olive to golden colored; posterior portions are blackish, often with a yellow band; wings are transparent with reddish-brown to blackish borders; legs are black; face has a black line that runs across the eye and down the side of the thorax

Below: as above but slightly paler

Sexes: similar

Egg: oval, light green, laid singly on host leaves

Larva: light green to yellow green to brown with pale, yellow spots, a small black spot on each abdominal segment, and a short, curved, yellow-based black horn off the rear

Larval Host Plants: various plants, including honeysuckle (*Lonicera* spp.), snowberry (*Symphoricarpos* spp.), and dogbane (*Apocynum* spp.)

Habitat: forest openings and margins, shrubby areas, meadows, old fields, parks, gardens, and urban areas

Broods: one to two generations; pupae overwinter

Abundance: occasional to common

Range: throughout

female

male

Compare: unique

Comments: This showy dimorphic species is arguably quite small compared to other giant silk moths. The adults are nocturnal and readily attracted to artificial lights. Their bold hindwing eyespots serve to startle a predator or deflect its attacker away from the insect's body. The distinctive larvae are gregarious and bear venomous defensive spines that deliver a painful burning sensation if touched. While initially alarming, the pain and irritation rarely last more than a few hours in most cases. Nonetheless, care should be taken when handling or working near the larvae. Fully grown larvae spin thick, dark-brown, papery, and leaf-wrapped cocoons that fall to the ground.

Io Moth
Automeris io

Family/Subfamily: Emperor, Royal, Moon, and Giant Silk Moths (Saturniidae)/Buck and Io Moths (Hemileucinae)

Wingspan: 2.0–3.0" (5.0–7.6 cm)

Above: male has yellow wings and a hairy body; forewing is mottled with brown; female has brown or reddish-brown to pinkish-brown forewings and a hairy body; hindwing is yellow with a large, round black eyespot bordered by black and red; inner hindwing margin has long red hairs; hindwing in female has some brown along the outer margin

Below: wings colored as above; forewing has round black eyespot; hindwing has faint central eyespot

Sexes: dissimilar; males are yellow and have larger, ferny antennae

Egg: oval, somewhat flattened, white, marked with yellow; laid in clusters on host leaves

Larva: bright green with red, a white lateral stripe, and numerous branched spines

Larval Host Plants: many different broadleaf trees and shrubs

Habitat: deciduous forests, wetlands, shrubby areas, parks, and yards

Broods: one to two generations; cocoons overwinter

Abundance: occasional to common

Range: mostly throughout; less common north and westward

Compare: unique

Comments: With a wingspan approaching seven inches, female
Imperial Moths are among the largest North American moths.
They are widely distributed across much of the eastern US
and southeastern Canada. The lovely adults vary considerably in pattern, with some being mostly yellow and others
significantly darker. Their robust larvae are even more variable in color, ranging from green to nearly chocolate brown.
Fully grown larvae do not spin a cocoon but instead pupate
underground. The species has experienced declines in some
regions likely due to a combination of light pollution, pesti-
cide use, and the nontarget impact of biocontrol agents.

Imperial Moth
Eacles imperialis

Family/Subfamily: Emperor, Royal, Moon, and Giant Silk Moths (Saturniidae)/Royal Moths (Ceratocampinae)

Wingspan: 3.5–7.0" (8.9–17.9 cm)

Above: highly variable; wings yellow marked with brown, reddish-brown, or purplish-brown spots, lines, or patches; each wing has a central dark eyespot

Below: generally as above but lighter and with more yellow

Sexes: similar, although females are more heavily patterned and often much larger

Egg: oval, cream, laid on host leaves

Larva: large and highly variable in color; green, dark brown, or reddish brown and covered with diffuse fine hairs; abdominal spiracles are marked with cream or yellow and resemble small eyespots; thorax bears four short, knobby horns

Larval Host Plants: numerous trees, including Sweetgum (*Liquidambar styraciflua*), maple (*Acer* spp.), oak (*Quercus* spp.), and pine (*Pinus* spp.)

Habitat: coniferous, mixed, and deciduous forests

Broods: one generation; pupae overwinter

Abundance: occasional to common

Range: southeastern portions of the region; rare or absent farther north and west

COMMONLY ENCOUNTERED CATERPILLARS

Butterfly and moth larvae are commonly known as caterpillars. As a group, caterpillars are perhaps as beloved as butterflies, but beyond a few notable examples (e.g. the brown woolly), many folks don't know how to identify them.

Here is a brief introduction to some of the caterpillars you're most likely to encounter in the Midwest.

Safety Note: Some caterpillars have obvious, showy bristles or spines for defense; some, such as the Io Moth caterpillar (page 381) can inflict a venomous sting. Complicating matters, not every "bristly" or "spiked" caterpillar is actually dangerous. (For some, it's an evolutionary ruse!) When in doubt, if you're not sure if a caterpillar is safe to handle, don't pick it up. Instead, if you must handle it, wear gloves.

American Dagger
Acronicta americana

Banded Woolly Bear
Pyrrharctia isabella (pg. 354)

Black Swallowtail
Papilio polyxenes (pg. 39)

Cecropia Moth
Hyalophora cecropia (pg. 369)

Common Buckeye
Junonia coenia (pg. 179)

Eastern Tent Caterpillar Moth
Malacosoma americanum

Io Moth
Automeris io (pg. 385)

Monarch
Danaus plexippus (pg. 299)

Mourning Cloak
Nymphalis antiopa (pg. 47)

Painted Lady
Vanessa cardui (pg. 277)

Spicebush Swallowtail
Papilio troilus (pg. 49)

Viceroy
Limenitis archippus (pg. 291)

SPECIES NOT INCLUDED

It was not possible to comprehensively cover every butterfly species found within the Midwest in this book. Therefore, the following list of butterflies includes those that are considered to be rare strays to the Midwest from other areas or are generally recorded only from the extreme (primarily the western or southern) periphery of the region. They are primarily known only from historic, isolated or very infrequent records. Nonetheless, they have the potential to be found within the region. It is likely that several other species will be added to this list in years to come, especially with the growing interest in butterfly watching.

Nysa Roadside-Skipper (*Amblyscirtes nysa*)

Oslar's Roadside-Skipper (*Amblyscirtes oslari*)

Texan Crescent (*Anthanassa texana*)

Western Green Hairstreak (*Callophrys affinis*)

Mead's Wood-Nymph (*Cercyonis meadii*)

Small Wood-Nymph (*Cercyonis oetus*)

Sagebrush Checkerspot (*Chlosyne acastus*)

Fulvia Checkerspot (*Chlosyne fulvia*)

Bordered Patch (*Chlosyne lacinia*)

Queen Alexandra's Sulphur (*Colias alexandra*)

Christina Sulphur (*Colias christina*)

Queen (*Danaus gilippus*)

Ancilla Blue (*Euphilotes ancilla*)

Rita's Blue (*Euphilotes rita*)

Chalcedon Checkerspot (*Euphydryas chalcedona*)

Mexican Yellow (*Eurema mexicana*)

Afranius Duskywing (*Erynnis afranius*)

Arrowhead Blue (*Glaucopsyche piasus*)

Dotted Skipper (*Hesperia attalus*)

Western Branded Skipper (*Hesperia colorado*)

Juba Skipper (*Hesperia juba*)

Pahaska Skipper (*Hesperia pahaska*)

Uncas Skipper (*Hesperia uncas*)

Green Skipper (*Hesperia viridis*)

Lupine Blue (*Icaricia lupini*)

Shasta Blue (*Icaricia shasta*)

Southern Pearly-Eye (*Lethe portlandia*)

Weidemeyer's Admiral (*Limenitis weidemeyerii*)

Ruddy Copper (*Lycaena rubidus*)

Common Mestra (*Mestra amymone*)

Leda Ministreak (*Ministrymon leda*)

Ridings' Satyr (*Neominois ridingsii*)

Simius Skipper (*Notamblyscirtes simius*)

California Tortoiseshell (*Nymphalis californica*)

Garita Skipperling (*Oarisma garita*)

Uhler's Arctic (*Oeneis uhleri*)

Ocola Skipper (*Panoquina ocola*)

Pale Swallowtail (*Papilio eurymedon*)

Old World Swallowtail (*Papilio machaon*)

Palamedes Swallowtail (*Papilio palamedes*)

Anise Swallowtail (*Papilio zelicaon*)

Rocky Mountain Parnassian (*Parnassius smintheus*)

Vesta Crescent (*Phyciodes graphica*)

Mylitta Crescent (*Phyciodes mylitta*)

Pale Crescent (*Phyciodes pallida*)

Painted Crescent (*Phyciodes picta*)

Field Crescent (*Phyciodes pulchella*)

Large Orange Sulphur (*Phoebis agarithe*)

Orange-barred Sulphur (*Phoebis philea*)

Margined White (*Pieris marginalis*)

Dotted Checkerspot (*Poladryas minuta*)

Long dash (*Polites mystic*)

Rhesus Skipper (*Polites rhesus*)

Sandhill Skipper (*Polites sabuleti*)

Appalachian Grizzled Skipper (*Pyrgus centaureae wyandot*)

Small Checkered-Skipper (*Pyrgus scriptura*)

Tailed Orange (*Pyrisitia proterpia*)

Callippe Fritillary (*Speyeria callippe*)

Coronis Fritillary (*Speyeria coronis*)

Edwards's Fritillary (*Speyeria edwardsii*)

Northwestern Fritillary (*Speyeria hesperis*)

Mormon Fritillary (*Speyeria mormonia*)

Zerene Fritillary (*Speyeria zerene*)

West Coast Lady (*Vanessa annabella*)

THE NAME GAME

As the interest in butterfly watching grows, so does the way that lepidopterists study and name butterflies. As in any discipline, not all lepidopterists agree unanimously on what every species should be called. In many cases, there simply hasn't been enough study to decisively classify a butterfly, and lepidopterists are still making discoveries, especially as technologies and techniques continue to improve. For the purposes of this guide, the scientific names listed follow ITIS, the Integrated Taxonomic Information System. Common names, however, are not standardized and tend to vary from one publication to another. The common names used in this book reflect those adopted by iNaturalist.

BUTTERFLY SOCIETIES AND OTHER RESOURCES

Organizations and societies are a great way to learn more about butterflies and moths in the Midwest. They also provide resources to make valuable contacts, share your enthusiasm and get out into the field.

The Lepidopterists' Society (www.lepsoc.org)

North American Butterfly Association (NABA)(www.naba.org)

The Illinois Butterfly Monitoring Network (https://ibmn.org)

Ohio Lepidopterists (www.ohiolepidopterists.org)

A variety of books, field guides and other digital resources are available to help grow your knowledge and enjoyment. In particular, various community scientist opportunities exist to contribute valuable data for scientific use, share your photographs, and secure species identifications. Here are a few of the most popular and useful.

Butterflies and Moths of North America
(www.butterfliesandmoths.org)

iNaturalist (www.inaturalist.org/)

Bugguide (https://bugguide.net)

North American Moth Photographer's Group
(https://mothphotographersgroup.msstate.edu)

Photo credits continued from page 4

Images used under license from Shutterstock.com. *(continued)*

Paul Reeves Photography: 15b, 16b, 44i, 50, 78, 126i, 128, 140, 158, 174, 174i, 192i, 206i, 222, 226i, 274i, 286i-2; 298i, 340, 344; **Martin Pelanek:** 226; **Dean Pennala:** 38i-1; **Carlos Pereira:** 280i; **gary powell:** 286i-1; **Rabbitti:** 17b; **Leena Robinson:** 18c; **samray:** 380; **Alan B. Schroeder:** 68; **Jennifer H. Seeman:** 20c; **Paul Sparks:** 16a, 216, 225; **Elizabeth Spencer:** 169; **TamiG:** 362; **Jim and Lynne Weber:** 20a, 53, 318, 326i; **Liz Weber:** 389c; **gregg williams:** 284i; **Wingman Photography:** 184i; **Wayne Wolfersberger:** 330; **Brian Woolman:** 19a; **Tom Worsley:** 388a; **yhelfman:** 76; **Rudmer Zwerver:** 15a

These images are used under the CC0 1.0 Universal (CC0 1.0) Public Domain Dedication, which is explained at https://creativecommons.org/publicdomain/zero/1.0/: **David Bird:** 192; **calinsdad:** 306; **Todd Eiben:** 296; **Robb Hannawacker:** 244; **Allan Harris:** 135, 235, 268; **jeffcherry:** 184; **Chrissy McClarren and Andy Reago:** 214; **ALAN SCHMIERER:** 139, 149; **Kim Selbee:** 162, 186; **Owen Strickland:** 198; **USFWS Midwest Region/Vince Cavalieri:** 93

These images are used under the Attribution 2.0 Generic (CC BY 2.0) license, which is available at https://creativecommons.org/licenses/by/2.0/: **Judy Gallagher:** 98, original image at https://www.flickr.com/photos/52450054@N04/27324756738/, 101, original image at https://www.flickr.com/photos/52450054@N04/33597794184/, 134, original image at https://www.flickr.com/photos/52450054@N04/49181873493/, 347 (altered), original image at https://www.flickr.com/photos/52450054@N04/6311116646/; **Melissa McMasters:** 96, original image at https://www.flickr.com/photos/cricketsblog/28439449830/

These images are used under the Attribution 4.0 International (CC BY 4.0) license, which is available at https://creativecommons.org/licenses/by/4.0/: **aarongunnar:** 34, original image at https://www.inaturalist.org/photos/20497302/, 251 (altered), original image at https://www.inaturalist.org/photos/154264379/, 292 (altered), original image at https://www.inaturalist.org/photos/23576984/; **Anne:** 63 (altered), original image at https://www.inaturalist.org/photos/81305482/; **Susan Blayney:** 242, original image at https://www.inaturalist.org/photos/8747367/, 346 (altered), original image at https://www.inaturalist.org/photos/175876844/; **Nick Block:** 57 (altered), original image at https://www.inaturalist.org/photos/3107904/, 71 (altered), original image at https://www.inaturalist.org/photos/18594626/, 72 (altered), original image at https://www.inaturalist.org/photos/2710945/, 110 (altered), original image at https://www.inaturalist.org/photos/3008137/, 168 (altered), original image at https://www.inaturalist.org/photos/19094554/, 219 (altered), original image at https://www.inaturalist.org/photos/19133700/; **Caleb Catto:** 182, original image at https://www.inaturalist.org/photos/135561909/; **Roy Cohutta Brown:** 70 (altered), original image at https://www.inaturalist.org/photos/153350127/, 297 (altered), original image at https://www.inaturalist.org/photos/234233304/, 326, original image at https://www.inaturalist.org/photos/234734157/; **drnancyjackson:** 86, original image at https://www.inaturalist.org/photos/209003858/; **Blair Dudeck:** 264, original image at https://www.inaturalist.org/photos/105499298/; **dvollmar:** 234 (altered), original image at https://www.inaturalist.org/photos/160209586/, 270, original image at https://www.inaturalist.org/photos/154248767/; **eamonccorbett:** 90, original image at https://www.inaturalist.org/photos/65051221/, 154, original image at https://www.inaturalist.org/photos/67998327/; **Nathan Earley:** 145, original image at https://www.inaturalist.org/photos/22690113/; **er-birds:** 282, original image at https://www.inaturalist.org/photos/93641965/; **Rob Foster:** 257, original image at https://www.inaturalist.org/photos/80573535/, 260, original image at https://www.inaturalist.org/photos/141047368/, 288 (altered), original image at https://www.inaturalist.org/photos/140252594/; **Judy Gallagher:** 52 (altered), original image at